The Politics of Drugs

Pressure Points in Irish Society

GENERAL SERIES EDITOR:
Professor Malcolm MacLachlan
Department of Psychology,
Trinity College Dublin

TITLES IN THE SERIES:

Cultivating Suicide? Destruction of Self in a Changing Ireland
by Caroline Smyth, Malcolm MacLachlan and Anthony Clare
(ISBN 1-904148-15-8)

The Politics of Drugs: From Production to Consumption
by Peadar King (ISBN 1-904148-19-0)

FORTHCOMING TITLES:

Refuge in Ireland: Myth and Reality
by Treasa Galvin

The Changing Face of Irish Authoritarianism
by Michael O'Connell

Pressure Points in Irish Society

The Politics of Drugs

From Production to Consumption

Peadar King

The Liffey Press

Published by
The Liffey Press Ltd
Ashbrook House, 10 Main Street
Raheny, Dublin 5, Ireland
www.theliffeypress.com

A catalogue record of this book is
available from the British Library.

ISBN 1-904148-19-0

Printed in the Republic of Ireland by Colour Books Ltd.

CONTENTS

ABOUT THE AUTHOR

Peadar King is an independent research consultant. Having worked as a second-level teacher for a number of years, he became involved in curriculum development research. European curriculum development projects in which he was involved addressed issues such as active ageing and promoting solidarity between the generations. He has worked on a number of gender educational initiatives and was co-ordinator of the Department of Education and Science's *Exploring Masculinities* programme. His recent research has focused on human rights and development education. He has a particular interest in international politics and global debt, topics on which he has produced film documentaries.

ACKNOWLEDGEMENTS

This report has its genesis in the evaluations conducted in 2000 and 2001 of sixteen Local Drugs Task Force projects in Cork and in work undertaken for the Limerick City-wide Drugs Strategy Initiative. Engagement with people in Cork and Limerick galvanised me to look again at my many assumptions about those who produce and consume illicit drugs. For challenging me to look again, I thank them.

In addition, I would like to thank: the National Drugs Task Force and The Cork Local Drugs Task Force for providing me with the opportunity of working with a team of committed and dedicated people in Cork City; members of the Limerick City-wide Drugs Strategy Initiative with whom I have worked; Rebecca Loughry and David Lane, former and current Cork Local Drugs Task Force Co-ordinator respectively and Willie Collins, Secretary to the Cork Local Drugs Task Force for their support and encouragement of me in this work and in my work as external evaluator for the Cork Local Drugs Task Force; Ann Kinsella, former librarian in Trócaire, and Patty Abozaglo of Trócaire who advised and helped me to source some of the reading that informed this discussion; Elizabeth Kiely, Department of Applied Social Studies, University College, Cork, for her detailed and thought-provoking comments on earlier drafts of this book; Gay/HIV Strategies for suggested readings; Mark Morgan, Head of Education, St Patrick's College, Drumcondra, Dublin for very encouraging and helpful comments when needed most; and at The Liffey Press, David Givens for his positive and encouraging remarks from receipt of first draft to final copy, and Brian Langan for forensic reading of later drafts.

A number of other people helped along the way and gave valuable, much-needed and deeply appreciated direction — to all, thanks. Finally, I wish to thank Orla O'Donovan and our daughters Sadhbh and Ríon for the tremendous encouragement and support to me in this and other endeavours.

As in all work of this kind, the usual convention that those named are not responsible for the content or indeed the quality of this discussion applies. For better or for worse, that responsibility is mine.

SERIES INTRODUCTION

The *Pressure Points in Irish Society* series presents concise critical commentaries on social issues of contemporary concern. These books are written to be accessible, topical and, if necessary, controversial. Their aim is to "add value" to social debate by highlighting neglected issues, developing new perspectives on an existing debate or presenting new data that can enlighten our thinking. Each of the topics addressed in the series in some sense challenges complacency, upsets a sense of social equilibrium or questions the status quo. In short, *Pressure Points* is concerned with those issues that suggest "everything is not OK".

The term "pressure point" can of course mean different things in different contexts. One meaning of a "pressure point" is an issue that can be targeted by political pressure or influence. However, for many important social issues, political pressure is often not mounted by those within the political establishment, but rather by specific pressure groups, non-governmental organisations, community actions or campaigning individuals. The reluctance of many politicians to "make an issue" out of problems such as drugs, suicide, disability or immigration — to name but a few — is probably because they see them as quagmires from which there is no easy exit; or perhaps more cogently, no easy "exit poll" for their political savvy to weigh up. Many of our most destructive social issues are quite simply not vote winners. In the sense of applying pressure in the body politic, then, *Pressure Points* hopes to highlight issues that have been insufficiently debated, or considered in a blinkered fashion.

Another meaning of "pressure point", in the "body physical", as it were, is a place on the body where an artery can be pressed against a bone in order to stop bleeding. This calls forth the spectre of a system haemorrhaging and needing acute intervention. Here, there is not only a sense of immediacy, but also of weakness in one system threatening the viability of the whole body. Systems theory, of course, conceptualises problems not as singular entities but as interconnected and mutually reinforcing or diminishing phenomenon. Such thinking is central to the practice of social sciences: problems need to be considered in a broad societal context, rather than being seen as discrete entities in isolated systems working away on their own.

While the Chinese wish "may you live in interesting times", we in Ireland certainly do. The advent of the so-called "Celtic Tiger" brought us economic prosperity undreamt of a mere decade earlier. The uneasy "Peace Process" has arrested the relentless and senseless demeaning of an island soaked in the blood of its intolerance. The hitherto unanticipated net migration into Ireland has transformed our image of an island to "leave from", to one of an island to "arrive at". This has presented us with new challenges and opportunities, not least the opportunity to see our own cultural conflict in a much broader perspective. As such, the call for pluralism in Ireland not only offers a warmer and more considered welcome to immigrants, but also a warmer and more considered welcome to the "others" within our island.

Alongside economic prosperity and the peace process, we have also experienced a decline in the iconography of traditionally significant social figures. Priests, doctors, politicians and other stalwarts of the social order have, at least as collective entities, fallen from a presumption of benevolence, propriety and public service. Some of our priests have abused the trust of a nation and raped the innocence of our children; many doctors (and others) extort fees for private consultations and in so doing further undermine the public services they are handsomely paid to provide; while some politicians have been found to be up to their necks in corruption. Such events have profoundly affected the presumption of living in a pro-social "civil" society. Collective identity and the fear of God have giving way to individuation and the fear of negative equity, in lives now mortgaged to the hilt. Economic success has congested our cities, recast our social values and provided a materialistic common denominator into which our "value" is being weighed up.

It is the nature of any rapidly changing society that while some social virtues are lost, others are gained. People now feel they

have greater civil liberties, greater access to the previously secret workings of the state, freedom to divorce, freedom to cohabit
and have children out of wedlock and recently (and perhaps most
dramatically), freedom to demonstrate their overwhelming wish
that our government not facilitate war. Ultimately, it is not change
per se that is good or bad, right or wrong, moral or immoral, but
how we adapt to our new circumstances. It has always been the
"job" of culture to make the lives of its members meaningful and
to offer them guidelines for living — feeling valued and having a
place in the world. The reach of globalisation, with its myriad
mechanisms, such as the internet, television, and retail outlets,
presents us afresh with the perennial challenge of deciding what
we are about. Yet this need for identity, for rootedness, occurs in
a completely new global context, with new "free trade" masters
in a world pulsating to corporate interests, in an enlarged European Union in which we will inevitably have less influence.

How we respond to the pressure points in Irish society will define who we are and what factors are most influential over us.
While a concern over how a small island like Ireland responds to
global challenges may seem to be rather a parochial concern, in
fact it is not. The world is made up of small communities with ethnic, religious and sometimes national identities. How local systems interact with global systems is of worldwide interest, as is
captured by that ugly term "globalisation". Our concerns in Ireland may well be particular, but how we adapt to global issues is
of general interest and importance. Many of the titles in this series
arise from the local presentation of issues of global import.

I am very pleased to be associated with The Liffey Press's
series on *Pressure Points in Irish Society*. We hope that in a modest way these books will advance thinking and practice in their
target areas and that you will enjoy reading them and be enli-
vened by them. Finally, I invite all interested parties, from all
walks of life, who have the drive to tackle such issues in a critical and concise manner, to join us by submitting a proposal to
myself or to The Liffey Press, for a future book in this series.

Malcolm MacLachlan,
Department of Psychology,
Trinity College Dublin.

*Dedicated to my mother and father, Margaret and Sean King —
who may or may not agree!*

Chapter 1

A DRUG-SATURATED WORLD

We are living in a drug-saturated world. An estimated 185 million people or 3.1 per cent of the world's population consume illicit drugs globally according to the UNODCCP (United Nations Office for Drug Control and Crime Prevention, 2002) and the number of people consuming prescribed drugs is growing apace. Monarchs, prime ministers, great writers and composers, wounded soldiers, overworked physicians, oppressed housewives, exhausted labourers, high-powered businessmen, playboys, sex workers, pop stars, stressed adolescents, defiant schoolchildren, happy young people, are listed in Davenport-Hines's (2001, p. *xi*) social history of drugs as among those who have used drugs.

All the indications are that, per head of population, Irish people too are significant consumers of illicit drugs. According to the UNODCCP, out of 23 Western European countries, Ireland has the highest consumption of ecstasy per head of population. Of those aged between 15 and 64, just fewer than 2.5 per cent took ecstasy at least once in the twelve months preceding the survey. The UK has the second highest at 1.6 per cent. Greece and Cyprus have the lowest rate at 0.1 per cent each.

In terms of cannabis consumption, Ireland and the UK share top spot with annual prevalence rates of 9.4 per cent of the population aged 15 and over. Ireland is third for cocaine consumption at 1.3 per cent of the population aged 15 and over, 0.4 per cent behind the UK and 0.2 per cent behind Spain. For opiate consumption, Ireland lies in shared ninth place along with five other countries with annual prevalence rates of 0.3 per cent but only 0.3 per cent behind the UK, Italy, Luxembourg and Portugal who have prevalence rates of 0.6 per cent.

While acknowledging that the measurement of illicit drug consumption is notoriously difficult given its clandestine nature, the figures do suggest that Ireland is, per head of population, a significant player in the field of illicit drugs. The above data are based on annual prevalence rates — the number of people who have consumed an illicit drug at least once in the last twelve months prior to being surveyed. The use of this measure is regarded as illustrative of real consumption patterns as opposed to lifetime prevalence — the number of people who have consumed drugs in their lifetime. A 60-year old person, for example, who smoked cannabis once when she was 19 does not present a real picture of current consumption levels.

However, measurement of illicit drug consumption does not, on its own, indicate the degree to which global society has, for whatever reason, come to depend on drugs. As the graph of illicit drug use has risen steadily in the last 30 to 40 years, so too has the graph of prescribed drugs. A random sample of the 2001 financial reports of nine pharmaceutical companies indicate sales of $210 billion with one pharmaceutical company claiming that its sales have increased exponentially each year for 69 consecutive years. Clearly, there is a growing demand for all sorts of drugs and there is no shortage of people willing to feed that demand.

Yet, considering this level of consumption, it seems that we know very little about drugs and their effects. A nationwide survey in Ireland, conducted by Bryan et al. (2000) on drug-related knowledge, attitudes and beliefs, suggests that as a society we have much to learn. Three-quarters of the survey respondents felt that the current drug situation was out of control. Approximately three-quarters believed all illegal drugs to be equally harmful, while over 40 per cent believed that people can become dependent on drugs after just one experience. Of greater concern, perhaps, is the finding that people feared and avoided drugs users and felt little or no sympathy for people with addictions. Over half the respondents felt that problem drug users had only themselves to blame (Bryan et al., 2000, pp. 24–35).

Ireland is not unique in this respect. Right across the EU, when it comes to illicit drugs, most Europeans share similar attitudes to the Irish (Flynn, 2001). In Ireland and in Europe, when it comes to the issue of drugs and, in particular, illicit drugs, it would appear that we are high on opinion and low on understanding.

THE PURPOSE OF THIS BOOK

Many of the factors that drive drug consumption also drive the production of and trade in illicit drugs. This account is concerned with examining the way in which attitudes and policies have evolved since some drugs came to be criminalised at the start of the twentieth century. Inevitably, such discussions become intertwined with broader discussions on international relations, neo-colonialism and war. Such considerations feature strongly in this work. The growth in drug consumption, particularly but not exclusively the growth of illicit drug consumption and the concomitant low level of understanding, provides the backdrop against which this book is set.

This account is written for people working in the drug prevention/harm reduction field. The evaluation of the Local Drugs Task Force Projects (Ruddle et al., 2000) suggests that many frontline workers need to locate and contextualise their work in current debates about drugs. Given that this is still a relatively new area of study, there is an ongoing need for practitioners and policy makers in this and related fields to be informed about these debates before embarking on any initiatives that seeks to address problematised or recreational drug use.

This book is also written for those who share a curiosity not just about drugs but also about global interconnectedness, neo-colonialism and human rights suppression/oppression. In particular, it seeks to examine the following questions:

- How did fear of difference and xenophobia come to influence the way in which some drugs were criminalised?

- How has the "war on drugs", which was first declared in 1972, become enmeshed with the "war on terrorism" and what has been the impact of that linkage on countries of the South and the South East?

- What are the key issues in the legalisation/(re)legalisation/ decriminalisation debate?

- What are the dominant perceptions of drug users?

- How have different social groups come to experience drug use?

- What strategies have policy makers and practitioners developed aimed at reducing drug-related harm or preventing drug use altogether?

FRAMING THE DEBATE

Consuming drugs of whatever sort and for whatever reason is nothing new, although the rate of consumption swiftly accelerated in the latter half of the last century. Dating back to antiquity, there is some evidence to suggest that the vast majority of cultures have sought ways and means of ingesting substances in the expectation that they would at best produce a feel-good factor or at worst go some way towards assuaging their pain and distress. Such experimentation would appear to have been openly tolerated and considered a normal part of the human condition until the early part of the last century when some drugs were government-sanctioned and others criminalised. Drug consumption had not yet become stigmatised, in a way that was to happen towards the end of the twentieth century, nor was it regarded as excessive or deviant behaviour.

Myth and misinformation, caricature and stereotype abound when it comes to discussions on drugs. Those involved in drugs — the producers, the traders and the consumers — are presented to the world as the *inhumane other*. The drug-created *other* is not unrelated to the creation of the race, class, disability and gender created *other* and so the whole issue of drugs has become entangled in an attempt to polarise, to dichotomise, to open up a world of *them and us*. And so the drug producer/ trader/user becomes tainted in public discourse.

Not only does the individual become tainted in the eyes of the morally resolute, but so too do many of the communities and the neighbourhoods where significant numbers of drug producers/dealers/users live. The pathology of the individual becomes a metaphor for the pathology of the ghetto or the pathology of the whole ethnic and racial group that is associated in popular perception with the drug trade, thereby cementing their outcast status. Unless, of course, the drug user comes from a solid middle class background, is attending university and is perceived as a future pillar of society — then the drug user is often regarded as going through a phase, sowing wild oats. And one doesn't lock up the sower and throw away the keys.

So the debate about drugs is intrinsically linked to the debate about power, about social and economic dominance, about class, about race, xenophobia and homophobia, about sexuality and gender — in essence, about difference. It is also about physical space, about the construction and subsequent abandonment of spaces where whole communities are ostracised and are left to live lives of long-term unemployment, educational exclusion, poverty and ramshackle housing.

Much of the debate on drugs that has taken place has been characterised by *closure* rather than *openness*. Reviewing the debate in Britain, Ross Coomber thinks it has been noteworthy for its shallowness and its tendency to concentrate on diametrically opposed arguments (1998, p. *xv*). Two polarised perspectives dominate: those who have no truck with drugs or with those who "ply their evil trade", and those who see intoxication as a human right and liberation from life's daily grind. Yet the need for more informed discussion is shared by many working in this area. Fergus McCabe, Chairperson of the Dublin-based Inter-Agency Drugs Project and the North Inner City Drugs Task Force has argued that "it is better to stimulate debate and discussion around contentious issues in an open and honest way rather than shy away from any controversy that might ensue" (McCabe, 1999, p. 1).

Trying to disentangle fact from fiction, substance from presentation and image from reality is central to engagement with this issue. Not only is the history of drugs clouded in smoke and distorted by mirrors, but so too is much of current policy. The evidence suggests that overt government policies are often undermined by its own covert actions. Yet such duplicity should not impugn the many genuine efforts to understand and respond. Not surprisingly, given the complexity of the issue involved, a divergence of views will always exist and competing perspectives on how policies should be framed will remain.

Trying to comprehend the multifarious dimensions of how drug policy has evolved to the present day involves trying to understand the historical, sociological, developmental and ethical dimensions of drugs as well as the pharmacological or epidemiological dimensions and their place in society. The social/economic/cultural/political context of drug use cannot be underestimated if one is ever to reach some level of understanding of this issue. Poverty, alienation and neglect of marginalised communities seem to be ever-present where problematic drug use exists. Certainly poverty, alienation, neglect and abuse of human rights drive drug production. Similarly, poverty, alienation, neglect and abuse of human rights drive community and personally debilitating drug consumption.

However, that is not the whole picture. For many people drug use does not appear to be problematic; rather it is part of their recreational world, a world that is not turned on its head by drug consumption. If drug consumption had that effect, then the estimated one-fifth of the EU population who are reported to have experimented with drugs would be in serious personal trouble, not to mention the 185 million people globally who have tried illicit drugs. Clearly, that is not the case. It is evident from a close examination of drug policies nationally and internationally that reductionist and simplistic arguments that all drug use inevitably leads to addiction only cloud any chance of understanding.

Any chance of understanding is further undermined by the polemic of the podium. This whole area is very conducive to simplistic, grandstanding, self-serving rhetoric that declares a "war on drugs". The very people who have been most prone to such declarations have, at least on occasion, been quite willing to illegally use drugs against their own people for geopolitical advantage. Pilger (1998), McCoy (1991) and Davenport-Hines (2001) all claim that the United States intelligence agency, the

CIA, was secretly involved in drug trafficking. That some have chosen to act so unethically does not take from the many who are genuinely opposed to any softening on the current prohibition.

FEAR AND THE OTHER

Much of the debate that has taken place has also been characterised by fear — fear of being caught offside, or at least not on the side of the righteous and the virtuous. And righteousness is never far removed from the debate — not the righteousness of the wounded but the righteousness of those who seek refuge in the rhetoric of prohibition. Party politicians of all persuasions have most keenly felt this fear: the left as well as the right has been keen to draw the infamous line in the sand. Furthermore, the space in which the debate has been conducted has been bedevilled by generalities, through the homogenisation of the drug user and producer as social outcasts.

In this space, the politics of identity and representation is very much in evidence. The drug producer/dealer/user is seen either as morally corruptible or morally defunct, to be feared or pitied or both. It is as if the vagaries of the human condition can be encapsulated and explained away in one or perhaps two safe if pithy declarations. This discussion seeks to go beyond such imposed limitations, beyond the paradigms of branded spaces and branded people.

The drug producer/dealer/user is further stigmatised, as will be seen as this discussion unfolds, as the stranger in our midst, threatening the very fabric of our society. When the drug user/trader/producer comes from outside the white European/ North American nexus, the threat is perceived as even greater; the stranger becomes the *dark* stranger. And naming and blaming the stranger in our midst is a very political act of exclusion.

In so far as people may have some sympathy for the plight of the producer and the consumer, seldom, if ever, does that sympathy and understanding extend to the dealer. Yet many dealers — as distinct from many international traffickers — experience the same level of rejection from mainstream society that is experienced by the producers and the consumers. For many dealers, their decision to resort to this form of capitalist

enterprise is rooted in their rejection from mainstream capitalism. They too have succumbed to the avaricious values of their
counterparts in what passes for the legitimate economy. Dealers too are deserving of some level of understanding, irrespective of how callously they may behave.

This discussion also seeks to go beyond what became
known in a different context as "the condemnation of the latest
atrocity". This discussion seeks to debunk the caricature of the
drug producer, the drug dealer and the drug user as mis-
guided, if not amoral, depraved individuals. It attempts to
probe the deep schisms that exist between those caught or who
are willing participants in the world of psychoactive illicit
drugs, and those who fulminate against them.

This account is written in an attempt to challenge the information and understanding deficit that exists. It is an attempt to move
the debate beyond the "who can think of the toughest measures?" paradigm. It is about openings rather than closures.
While the primary focus of this work is about illicit drugs, it is
also about how we understand, relate to and accommodate difference, how we move from closed debate to open exploration.

POWER, POLITICS AND DRUGS

The current general discursive framework, on this and related
issues, is very Western and Euro-centred and writing from the
point of view of the producers is an attempt at counterbalancing
that dominant view. In general, the Southern perspective is un-
heard and unheeded in this and other areas in the Northern
Hemisphere.

Adopting such a perspective invariably brings one into conflict with the dominant geopolitical narrative that dictates all
North-South discussions. In this narrative, geographical identities and state self-determination are regarded as subservient to
the political needs of their larger neo-imperial neighbouring
powers. These powers believe they have the right to exert
whatever political and economic influence on their small
neighbours that they wish. In the context of the United States'
relationships with its neighbours in Central and South America,
independent thought and political engagement outside the dic-

tums of capitalist orthodoxy is proscribed. To comment or question that imposition in the aftermath of the events of 11 September 2001 is to invoke the false, lazy but achingly predictable knee-jerk reaction, and indeed accusation, of being anti-American or anti-British. Such accusations are, in reality, thinly disguised attempts to censor and silence. The swagger and confidence of the "silence the dissenter" brigade has grown apace since 11 September 2001.

To assert deficiencies, inadequacies and inappropriateness in a particular government's policies or to point out breaches of international law does not in any way imply that one is intent on demonising the population of that particular country. Many of the policies pursued by governments are done so without the consent or knowledge of its people.

Noam Chomsky clearly differentiates between government policies and its citizens. Reviewing a series of policies in relation to terrorism, Chomsky (1989) argues that many policy initiatives do not have the consent of a majority of the people and where they do, that consent is often secured through a sophisticated process of manipulation, control of information and the dissemination of disinformation. To put it another way, consent is achieved through careful and calculated propaganda. When that fails, the good of the people or world peace or the threat of terrorism is invoked. Finding some aspects of a country's policies and values unacceptable and unjust does not preclude the possibility of celebrating other values and policies.

To question global economic injustice in the aftermath of the atrocities of 11 September 2001 must remain an option; otherwise the forces of terrorism will have won out.

STRUCTURE OF THE BOOK

And so, why the title, *The Politics of Drugs: From Production to Consumption*? The initial decision to criminalise some drugs was a very political act. It was rooted in racism and xenophobia and racism and xenophobia remain barely concealed justifications for current drug policies. Woodiwiss (1998), Mott and Bean (1998), Bourgois (1995), Davenport-Hines (2001) and Haskins (2003) chronicle the way in which drug scaremongering was and continues to be racially tinged. The issues that affect production are also in many cases the issues that drive consumption and this account is interested in highlighting that relationship. The section on production is written primarily from the perspective of the producers while the perspective of the consumer remains a constant throughout.

Despite the enormous impact that illicit drug production has had on global relations in the last century, but more particularly in the last 40 years, much of the current discussions are confined to the "defective human being" model. A greater curiosity is needed. A greater knowledge based on empirical research is needed that will open up the discussion and move it beyond the level of stereotype. A curiosity is needed that extends beyond seeing drug users as defective human beings and drug producers as Third World exploiters of First World fallibility.

Chapter Two attempts to locate the drug industry and the debate in an international context. Given the pre-eminence of the United States as the sole remaining superpower, and given that it has now four decades of experience of the "war on drugs" behind it, this discussion starts with an exploration of its drug policies. These policies have repercussions far beyond US borders. In particular, United States policies have had severe repercussions for a number of South American countries, particularly Colombia, Peru and Bolivia. The "war on drugs" that was first declared by former president Richard Nixon has since then become enmeshed with the "war on terrorism" that has come to dominate United States foreign policy since the atrocities that were committed on 11 September 2001. This account attempts to explore the connection between the two wars.

Chapter Two also examines EU policies, policies that are, in the main, significantly different to those of the United States. Britain's policy was, at least up to recently, more akin to US policy and at odds with the general drift of policy in member states of the EU. This chapter traces the contrasting development of British and Dutch drug policies. The chapter concludes with an overview of Irish policy. In summary, this chapter attempts to come to some understanding regarding how some drug use came to be criminalised in the past 100 years and how that criminalisation has impacted on the producer and the consumer.

Chapter Three examines the conjunction between social class, ethnicity, race, gender, sexual orientation, age and drug use. In order to understand the dynamic of drug use fully, the chapter will also attempt to profile users and the social, economic, ethnic, class, racial and environmental conditions that impact on increased use and responses to the drug "problem".

Chapter Four details a range of different types of interventions that have been developed to counter or reduce the adverse effects of drug use. In outlining responses that have been put in place, two major approaches can be identified, namely abstinence and harm reduction. These two approaches will frame the review of policy initiatives in this area.

Chapter Five, in reflecting on preceding chapters, summarises key issues and draws some tentative conclusions.

In attempting to make some sense of these very complex and difficult issues, this account deliberately eschews any individualistic rationalisations that apportion blame on the poor, on minority ethnic groups, on prisoners, on women, on gay men. This book is not about personal failures and inadequacies. Nor does it seek to psychologically pathologise people whose lives have been ravaged by addictive drug use as deficient individuals. Rather, this book seeks to challenge the ideology that underpins the current war on drugs and the related war on terrorism. It seeks to identify the structural conditions, and the political forces that have created the drug-induced chaos that characterises far too many people's lives.

THE LANGUAGE OF DRUGS

But first, the issue of language. The language of drugs has an importance that might not initially be appreciated. The language of drugs, according to MacGregor (1999, p. 77), and the way in which terms like use and misuse are used and interpreted is important as it reflects particular sets of values. Van Muijlwijk describes this as the "naming, framing and reframing" (1999, p. 38) task. Naming and framing is of central importance in the understanding of any issue and involves exploring questions like the following: What is the broad context in which this debate is being conducted? What precise meanings, if any, do people attach to the language they use? Is the discursive model too restrictive and is there a need to reframe the debate to move it on to other ground?

According to Kiely and Egan (2000, p. 7), the terms *use* and *misuse* reflect particular value judgements and lack clear meaning. They argue that the term "use" is used in the context that some drug use is acceptable and prevention of all drug use is "neither desired nor intended". In contrast, the term "misuse" reflects a bias against drug taking and "tends to be applied when referring to drug consumption which has become more frequent or more chaotic". However, Kiely and Egan stress that these concepts are not clearly defined despite the ideological baggage attached to them. Walton argues that the language of the debate is dominated by "admonition, prohibition and stern judgement" (2001, p. x). In an attempt to remain true to the spirit of openness in the discussion on drugs, and in recognition of the baggage that is attached to terms like "misuse" and "abuse", the terms "use" and "user" will be used throughout this discussion. But people who use drugs are not just "drug users". There is a lot more to each person's life than one attribute. Yet people who use drugs are often referred to as just "drug users" as if that were the sum total of their lives. The net result of using is a diminution of the person's identity to that of one aspect of their personhood. This diminution is much more likely to be applied to younger people of working class origins than to older people or to young people from more advantaged sections of society.

Chapter 2

THE "WAR ON DRUGS"

INTRODUCTION

There was much concern and "moral panic"[1] (Kiely and Egan, 2000, p. 77) at the increase in drug use in Ireland in the latter part of the last decade. While the scale and intensity of drug consumption in the 1980s in Dublin in particular was of a different order to what preceded this period, the moral panic that ensued proved to be a very poor basis for response. That remains very much the picture, but the reality is that substance use has been part not only of Irish history but of human experience globally since ancient times. This chapter will attempt to chart that reality by addressing the following questions:

- Historically, to what extent have the use of psychoactive agents been part of the human condition?

- What role, if any, does drug production play in global capitalist production?

- What has been the impact of the United States government's declared "war on drugs"?

- What has been the response of the EU to the escalation of drug consumption and in what way has that policy differed from that of the United States?

---

[1] Goode and Ben-Yehuda, cited in Karim Murji (1998), describe moral panic as "a heightened level of concern, increased hostility towards those associated with the activity, a high level of consensus that the activity is a real and serious threat, exaggeration of the nature of the threat and volatility of moral panics" (1998, p. 76).

- What have been the major influences in British drug policy and how has that policy evolved in the last ten years?

- In what way has Dutch drug policy been regarded as pioneering?

- What are the key elements in current Irish drug policy?

HISTORICAL CONTEXT

The use of drugs as psychoactive or mind-changing agents is believed to date back to antiquity. According to McCoy et al. (1996, p. *viii*) the use of opium dates back at least to the Ancient Greeks and references to marijuana appear in early Persian, Hindu, Greek, Arab and Chinese writings. Homer's *Odyssey* tells of how Helen sought to comfort and console those who grieved for the dead warriors of the Trojan War in the twelfth century BC:

> Into the bowl in which their wine was mixed, she slipped a drug that had the power of robbing grief and anger of their sting and banishing all painful memories. No one who had swallowed this dissolved in wine could shed a single tear that day even for the death of his mother and father, or if they put his brother or his own son to the sword. (Davenport-Hines, 2001, pp. 8–9)

Davenport-Hines (2001) claims that Helen's concoction was "probably a solution of opium and alcohol". Walton (2001) dates opium use from 8000 BC. Heroin is derived from the opium poppy, *papaver somniferum*, which contains the alkaloid morphine, and it originates in the Mediterranean area. Like the coca plant, it had medicinal and pain-relieving properties. Not only was it used medically but the "dreamlike state induced by inhaling the smoke of its congealed and dried sap appears to have been among the very earliest examples of systematic intoxication in human history, almost certainly predating alcohol" (Walton, 2001, p. 111).

Archaeological evidence of poppy capsules has emerged from excavations of Neolithic sites in Germany, Switzerland, Austria and Romania (Davenport-Hines, 2001, pp. 2–18).

Charred pipes thought to have been used in the smoking of opium have been excavated in Spain, dating to 4200 BC, and in Cyprus, dating to 1200 BC (Walton, 2001). Walton claims that intoxication held a privileged place in certain rituals in Ancient Greece. Alcohol was both a social lubricant in the symposium and wine was central to the "sacrament of the orgiastic worship of Dionysus" (Walton, 2001, p. *xxv*). While many members of the symposium were imbibing with abandon, they were less indulgent of the masses who were drinking in the taverns and whose consumption did not have the intellectual bases that justified their own consumption.

With the exception of the Inuit people (formerly known as Eskimos) who were unable to grow any raw material that might produce mind-altering substances, Walton (2001) and Butler (2002) claim that every society has used psychoactive substances. It is even claimed that drugs were used by Neanderthals. Haskins (2003, pp. 19–20) claims reports on the excavation of a 60,000-year-old Neanderthal grave site at Shanidar in Iraq where plants were found beside a male skeleton. The plant, woody horsetail or *ephedra vulgaris*, has stimulant properties similar to those of amphetamines or ecstasy. The practice of using mind-changing drugs for pleasure or as a means of coping with stress and anxiety is "ancient and almost universal" (Butler, p. *vii*). When the Spanish conquistadors lurched into the Inca Empire in 1531, the chewing of coca had been part of local practice for centuries (McCoy et al., 1996). Davenport-Hines (2001, p. 6) reproduces the following colonialist account from the Italian explorer Amerigo Vespucci (1454–1512) of Inca consumption of coca:

> They had their mouths full of leaves of a green herb, which they continually chewed like beasts . . . each had around his neck two dry gourds, one full of that herb and the other full of white flour. . . . the thing seemed wonderful, for we did not understand the secret, or with what object they did it.

The CIIR (Catholic Institute for International Relations, 1991) estimate that coca was part of the staple diet of many indigenous people in an area stretching from Central America to the Southern tip of the Andes for approximately 6,500 years.

By the early eighteenth century, there is evidence to suggest that opium had been introduced into England. By the middle of that century, Chinese labourers introduced the practice of opium smoking into England. By the end of the eighteenth century it was possible to isolate cocaine from the coca leaf and the use of cocaine became popular among the aristocracy. The end of the eighteenth century also marked the introduction of heroin into England. However, if the twentieth century closed with what is popularly perceived as a drugs epidemic, the opening of the century saw an actual decline in the use of psychoactive drugs. Furthermore, by the end of the twentieth century, drug use had become heavily criminalised; at the start of the century, all drugs were controlled but legal.

In Ireland, alcohol was the primary substance that was traditionally used to generate an altered state. Fr James Cullen founded the Pioneer Total Abstinence Association in Dublin in 1898. He did so in response to what was perceived as a major problem with alcohol consumption. Another Catholic priest, Fr Theobald Mathew, had initiated a temperance movement in the 1840s but his efforts did not survive beyond his own lifetime. Indeed, Irish literature (Frank McCourt's *Angela's Ashes*, Marian Keyes's *Rachel's Holiday* and Edna O'Brien's *Girl with Green Eyes* to name but three) provides vivid testimony of the consequences of alcohol abuse. In terms of drug use, Ireland was a late developer. It is now a truism to say that the 1960s did not happen in Ireland until the 1970s. Experimentation with various illegal substances that had taken root in other countries in the 1960s and 1970s did not become part of the Irish streetscape until the 1970s and the 1980s. When it hit, the complacent belief that it could not happen in Ireland cracked and policy at all levels was caught unprepared for the scale of the drug use that was about to hit the streets. According to O'Mahony (1996, p. 40), the Irish drug problem (read heroin) "sneaked up on a complacent and naïve Irish society, which was ignorant of the nature of the modern, urban, opiate drugs subculture which believed itself immune to its worst excesses".

DRUGS AS A CULTURAL PHENOMENON

The 1960s and the 1970s witnessed an upsurge in drug use. The first national survey on drugs in the United States (1967) reported that "marijuana was becoming a common form of recreation for many middle and upper class college youths and in the affluent areas" (Harrison and Pottieger, 1996, p. 10). Drugs also became associated with particular forms of music and with particular life-styles, a trend that is still evident today. The 1960s mods, dressed in black suits and drainpipe trousers, cane in hand or driving a scooter, were strongly linked with amphetamines. The punk era of the 1970s was also associated with amphetamines. Ecstasy became available in the late 1980s in the United States. The emergence of ecstasy as the preferred drug of choice of many young people is linked to the emergence of rap culture from the black ghettos of the US and the northern dance clubs in England. Later, despite some high profile deaths, the more mainstream dance scene adopted it. Dance drugs are associated with clubs that define themselves as house, hard house, acid house, drum 'n' bass, jungle, garage, techno, trance and rave, according to the London Drug Policy Forum (1996).

The growth of the drug culture was, according to MacGregor (1999, p. 71), interwoven with the cultural revolutions of the 1960s and 1970s, a culture she describes as "hedonistic, challenging and exhibiting declining respect for authority". Since the 1960s and the 1970s, drug use has become normalised, or at the very least a process of normalisation is under way, and has become what Shapiro (1999, p. 18) calls "an unremarkable part of the lifestyle kit". South (1999, p. 3) goes on to claim that experimentation with or use of drugs has become "closely woven into the experimental and cultural fabric of 'ordinary' life". Non-acquaintance with drugs, South (1999) claims, has become the deviation from the norm.

Some commentators argue that the desire for intoxication transcends all social classes and social conditions. From the time of the Ancient Greeks and Romans, right up to the twentieth century prohibitionist movement in the United States and the "war on drugs", many have found ways to circumvent the abolitionists.

Walton (2001) argues that some of those who publicly supported the prohibition on alcohol consumption were not only
drinking alcohol themselves but were involved in bootlegging.
He claims that during the presidency of Warren Harding, "prohibition's first president" (2001, p. 140), the White House was

> awash with bootleg hooch. Part of the Senate library had
> been curtained off, and had become "the best bar in town",
> well stocked thanks to regular visits from ingratiatingly sub-
> servient customs officials bringing with them confiscated
> liquor. (Walton, 2001, pp. 140–1)

In the post (alcohol) prohibitionist era, former US President Bill
Clinton tried to distinguish between smoking and inhaling, ad-
mitting to smoking but not inhaling dope. The younger George
Bush declined during the presidential election to say whether
or not he experimented with illicit drugs. "Maybe I did, maybe
I didn't" (Haskins, 2003, p. 181) was the only reply he would
make. Things are not always what they appear to be.

Drugs are now perceived by many commentators to be a
"normal" part of society although there remains stiff opposition
to the normalisation thesis. The normalisation thesis was given
strong impetus by Noel Gallagher of Oasis who claimed in an
interview in *New Musical Express* in 1997 that taking drugs was
like getting up and having a cup of tea — which ironically contains the drug caffeine — in the morning (Shiner and Newburn,
1999, p. 123).

Gallagher was not, of course, the first rock star to admit to
taking drugs, nor was drug consumption confined to rock music. Davenport-Hines (2001, pp. 330–331) and Haskins (2003,
pp. 231–242) include people like Paul McCartney, John Lennon,
Johnny Cash, Elvis Presley, Jimi Hendrix, Jim Morrison, Keith
Moon, Louis Armstrong, Charlie Parker, Sid Vicious, Brian
Jones, Keith Richards, Janis Joplin, Bob Dylan, Kurt Cobain and
Hank Williams in a list of those who have admitted to having
experimented with drugs. Some of the above paid dearly with
their lives for their experimentation and consumption. Brian
Jones, Jimi Hendrix, Janis Joplin and Jim Morrison all died between 1969 and 1970, coincidentally at the age of 27. Other
high-profile deaths were to follow.

Many of their songs — from Dylan's assertion that "every-body must get stoned" in *Rainy Day Women #12 & 35* to The Beatles' admission that "I get high with a little help from my friends" or their dreamy idyll of "picture yourself in a boat on a river with tangerine trees and marmalade skies" in *Lucy in the Sky With Diamonds* — celebrate the use of psychoactive sub-stances. What was different about Gallagher's admission that he used drugs to similar assertions by those who preceded him was that there was no public outcry. He even received support in many unlikely quarters. Unlike when Mick Jagger was ar-rested in 1967, for possession of four amphetamine tablets, Gal-lagher's admission was not marked by editorials in *The Times* about "hedonistic behaviour". However, the tolerant attitude towards drug use among rock stars did not extend to the boy-band phenomenon that dominated pop music in the latter half of the 1990s. The reaction to East 17 member Brian Harvey, who endorsed the drug ecstasy in January 1997, was less indulgent than in the case of Noel Gallagher. Harvey was fired.

It would appear that the sentiments expressed by both Gal-lagher and Harvey are shared by many of their age group and that this view transcends social class background. Social class differences have "virtually disappeared", at least when it comes to cannabis and ecstasy, and the use of illegal and legal substances have become "enmeshed with each other in the so-cial space of young people" (Morgan, 2001, p. 50). The nor-malisation process is, in keeping with its musical (and other) proponents, in full swing.

In other literary genres, the normalisation thesis has also been explored. Irvine Welsh attracted much literary criticism for his account of heroin addiction in his novel and subsequent film *Trainspotting*. Notwithstanding his painfully graphic depic-tion of heroin addiction, he was excoriated by many critics as glamorising drug use and celebrating the dark elements of hu-man existence. Fiachra Gibbons quotes Ronald Frame in *The Guardian* newspaper as describing Welsh's writing as "clichéd brand novels celebrating such dark subjects as cannibalism, necrophilia and sado-masochism" (Gibbons, 2001). One online reviewer described his work as follows: "the whole thing stinks of a cynical attempt at whipping together elements of pop culture, pop music and the popularisation of the serious issue of heroin abuse and I hate it" (dooyoo, 1996). Whether Welsh may have contributed to the normalisation of heroin consumption in his book remains a moot point, but he certainly did not glamorise it:

> Ah soon started tae feel fucking shan n aw. Bad cramps wir beginning tae hit us as we mounted the stairs tae Johnny's gaff. Ah wis dripping like a saturated sponge, every step bringing another gush fae ma pores. Sick Boy wis probably even worse, but the cunt was beginning no tae exist fir us. Ah wis only aware ay him slouching tae a halt oan the bannister in front ay us, because he wis blocking ma route tae Johnny's and the skag. He wis struggling fir breath, haudin grimly oantay the railing, looking as if he wis gaunnae spew intae the stairwell. (Welsh, 1999, p. 6)

Irvine Welsh was not the first writer to graphically describe the ill-effects of drug taking. Thomas De Quincey (1785-1859), the author of *The Confessions of an English Opium Eater* and according to Davenport-Hines (2001) the first European to consciously take a drug for its feel-good sensations as opposed its pain-relieving attributes, wrote about the horrors and nightmares he experienced:

> I was stared at, hooted at, grinned at, chattered at, by monkeys, by paroquets, by cockatoos. I ran into pagodas and was fixed for centuries at the summit, or in secret rooms; I was the idol; I was the priest; I was worshipped; I was sacrificed. Thousands of years I lived and was buried in stone coffins, with mummies and sphinxes, in narrow chambers at the heart of eternal pyramids. I was kissed, with cancerous kisses, by crocodiles and was laid, confounded with all unutterable abortions, amongst reeds and Nilotic mud. (Quoted in Davenport-Hines, 2001, p. 42)

ILLICIT DRUGS IN A CAPITALIST ECONOMY

The growing acceptance that drugs are part and parcel of "normal" life marks the blurring between legal and illegal trade and the fracturing of any type of authority that seeks to establish clear lines of demarcation between what is considered legal and what is considered illegal. Proponents of the normalisation thesis argue that the illegality of the drug trade is not that dissimilar to the exploitation of under-age textile workers that produce for the more glamorous fashion designer houses. Officially, both are not tolerated yet both play an indispensable role in capitalist production and consumption. Esperanza's film documentary *Race to the Bottom* chronicles how exploitative labour is central to the textile industry and how it ensures that those of us in the western world can have easy access to relatively cheap clothing. The illicit drugs trade and the illicit production of cheap textiles make vast sums of money for relatively small numbers of people at the expense of huge numbers of people.

Butler (2002) argues that the growth in the drug trade is "just one example of the wider phenomenon of globalisation" (2002, p. 1). International trade in illicit drugs at the end of the twentieth century matched that in arms and oil. Dixon (1998, pp. 6, 42) and Davenport-Hines (2001, p. *ix*) estimate that the current drug trade is worth $400 billion dollars or 8 per cent of all international trade. Drug trading is, he says, a "world-class, highly profitable mega industry, a huge mass market retail operation". In the language of economics "the risk/reward ratio" (*First Report of the Ministerial Task Force to Reduce the Demand for Drugs*, 1996, p. 6) is a sufficiently attractive incentive for the international criminal community to remain in business. And the rewards are significant.

A batch of heroin worth €1,000 in Afghanistan, for example, is worth €11,000 in Turkey, €24,000 in the Netherlands and up to €101,000 in Ireland (National Drugs Strategy 2001–2008, p. 66). Bourgois (1995) claims it costs approximately $8 to $10 to produce an ounce of pure powder cocaine and that the same ounce has a market value of $2,000 once it is adulterated and packaged into $10 quart gram vials — returning an extraordinary profit margin of 99.5 per cent. The international trade in drugs is currently worth more than the combined GDP of Germany and Canada (Dixon, 1998).

While the degree to which drug consumption in the western "developed" world is wholly linked to poverty is highly con-

tested, there is clear evidence that poverty and oppression play a pivotal influence in enabling the global drugs trade to flourish. Poverty and oppression drive particular kinds of consumption, most notably heroin, and crack and poverty and oppression drive production. Alan García, the former President of Peru, has argued that the drug trade is the only successful multinational in Latin America. Because of the way trade is monopolised and controlled by western transnational companies in the key areas of coffee and banana production, poor farmers of South America and Afghanistan have no other recourse but to produce for the drug trade, if they are to eke out any minimal existence. They have no option but to produce for the illegal market if they are to survive.

While the current model of capitalism forces people into the production of illicit drugs, historically, these very same drugs were used to drive capitalist production in the sixteenth and seventeenth centuries. Davenport-Hines (2001) claims that the Spanish *conquistadors* used coca to expand output by increasing productivity. The indigenous peoples were forced to work in silver mines under extraordinarily difficult conditions at an altitude of nearly 14,000 feet. A handful of leaves enabled them to survive without meat for days. Coca made them more compliant and a compliant workforce is a huge asset for any capitalist endeavour. In the twentieth century, the production of coca continues to play a pivotal role in capitalist production.

Cocaine production from the coca plant is concentrated in war-torn Colombia, in debt-ridden Bolivia, the poorest country in Latin America, and in Peru, once a pariah country in the world of international money markets. The Bolivian government estimates that half a million of its citizens are involved in cultivating, processing and transporting coca and its derivatives. Bolivia can produce between 10,000 and 150,000 metric tonnes of coca leaves annually. Not all of this is produced for the drugs trade and not all of it is illegal. Some of the leaves are chewed and some are used to make coca wines or tea, both of which are useful antidotes to high altitudes. Bolivia's former finance minister Flavio Machicado has argued that "there would be social and economic catastrophe here . . . if narcotics were to disappear overnight, we would have rampant unemployment, there would be open protest and violence" (George, 1992, p. 41).

Economist.com estimates that Colombia earns between $2.5 and $5 billion or 2–4 per cent of Gross Domestic Product (GDP) in repatriated income from illicit drugs. In a poor country with few opportunities, that is a significant sum. While this money is primarily earned from the production of coca, heroin production has emerged in the high Andean slopes in the south of the country.

Heroin production is now concentrated mainly in Southwest Asia with the bulk of production — at least up 1999/2000 — coming from Afghanistan and the dictatorially ruled Burma[2] (*Irish Times*, 21 February 2001). Heroin production was actually in decline prior to the war on Afghanistan in 2001/2002 and the decline was verified by the United Nations Drug Control Programme (UNODCCP). On 10 September 1997, the Taliban Ministry of Foreign Affairs issued the following declaration.

> The Islamic State of Afghanistan informs all compatriots that as the use of heroin and hashish is not permitted in Islam, they are reminded once again that they should strictly refrain from growing using and trading in hashish and heroin. Anyone who violates this order shall be meted out a punishment in line with the lofty Mohammed and Sharia law and thus shall not be entitled to launch a complaint. (Transnational Institute, 2002, p. 7)

The initial response was unimpressive despite the Taliban's bloody reputation for dealing with dissent. The 1998/99 winter production reached record levels. An estimated 4,565 tons of opium were produced in that season from 90,583 hectares (UNODCCP, 2002, p. 47). In September 1999, just before the new planting season, Mullah Omar issued a decree to decrease poppy cultivation by one-third. UN monitors confirmed that production did decrease by 28 per cent, down to 3,276 tons. Mullah

---

[2] The Nobel Peace laureate Aung San Suu Kyi and the democratic movement of Burma have requested that the name Burma be retained in reference to their country despite the name change to Myanmar imposed by the military regime that currently controls the country.

Omar followed the September 1999 declaration with a total ban in July 2000. Several arrests and destruction of fields followed.

The Afghan opium economy experienced "a spectacular crash" (TNI, 2002, p. 8) following on from the edict. By May 2001, opium had almost completely disappeared in the Taliban controlled areas of Afghanistan. Final results showed for the year 2001 that an estimated 7,606 hectares of opium were cultivated, down 91 per cent from the previous year with a corresponding reduction in output of 96 per cent (UNODCCP, 2002, p. 47). Ironically, in areas controlled by the Northern Alliance, opium production was flourishing. Prior to the ban on opium cultivation, the total value of the Afghan crop has been estimated at about $200 million a year (World Drugs Report, 2000, p. 7). TNI's estimates for 1999 are higher at $251 million but they estimate that this figure had fallen to $91 million by 2000 and to $56 million by 2001. Most of the $56 million was earned and taxed in Northern Alliance-controlled territory.

The dramatic drop in production was not, however, without grave consequences. The World Food Programme (WFP) concluded that the ban resulted in a severe loss of income for an estimated 3.3 million people. This figure includes 80,000 farm families totalling 480,000 people plus 480,000 itinerant labourers and their families, totalling 2.8 million people. Inevitably, these people, when given the opportunity were always going to return to the production of the one crop that would yield an income and so since the war on Afghanistan, production of opium has almost returned to pre-1999 levels. The expected production for 2002 is between 1,900 and 2,700 metric tons, about two-thirds of the 2000 yield (UNODCCP, 2002, p. 41). Less than a year after the war on Afghanistan, it was clear that Afghan farmers had resumed opium production, thereby undermining one of the justifications for the war, namely that the production of opium would be eradicated once and for all. The reality is that the opposite is the case.

Thus, it is clear that poverty and exclusion are the driving forces of drug production in Southeast Asia and in South America. Equally, many argue, at the end of the cycle in the streets and cities of Ireland and elsewhere, the drug trade is heavily though by no means wholly dependent on poverty for its existence. The *First*

Report of the Ministerial Task Force on Measures to Reduce the Demand for Drugs, which focused on heroin misuse, concluded that unemployment, poor living conditions and general disadvantage were strong predictors of heroin use. The strong correlation between poverty and drug use has also been highlighted by the Combat Poverty Agency, which has referred to the "irrefutable evidence of the strong link between poverty and drug use" (2001, p. 2). The likelihood of seriously eroding the grip that some drugs, particularly heroin, have on people living in impoverished neighbourhoods without addressing the underlying poverty is remote. Such predictors were deep-seated and intergenerational. Generation after generation, many families and whole communities have felt locked out of mainstream society.

These families and communities typified the reserve army of labour that could be mobilised in times of economic expansion and then summarily dismissed in more lean times. They were little more than fodder for a capitalist system. However, they were not unaware of or inured from the changes that were happening around them. They may very well have been pushed aside by the demands of capitalism and by a state that repeatedly and systematically ignored them. They too were told that they were different, they too were "othered". They may not be able to graduate from the best of schools or be in a position to cut deals on land or shares but they were beginning to understand that there were other ways of cutting a deal.

Some families fought back. Drug-dealing provided an alternative capitalist system from which they could achieve the kind of riches that other individuals in society were enjoying. Their drug-dealing was a statement of defiance against a state that did not care and against a system within which they would never be regarded as equals. Their social capital would never find acceptance in mainstream capitalist workplaces so they systematically created their own capitalist system that was no less avaricious and no less corrupt. Their world was a microcosm of the bigger world. Their world was as patriarchal as the mainstream system. Their world was as corrupt as was the mainstream.

Drug-dealing offered a way out poverty and marginalisation and a way of fulfilling their entrepreneurial drive. It offered a means whereby they could get their hands on some of the status symbols, the cars, the houses, the horses, the holidays that society's elites had so jealously guarded. The pity was that such defiance against the capitalist system had such tragic consequences. In taking on the role of dealer and trafficker, they further exploited their own, other poor people. What separated them from the macro-capitalist system was that their exploitation was conducted on the doorstep of the so-called developed world. Such flagrant public exploitation offends First World sensibilities. Mainstream capitalist exploitation is more hidden and consequently more acceptable — at least to the eyes of Western world consumers — in factories, farms and households in countries like Bangladesh, India, The Philippines, Brazil and Côte d'Ivoire, to name but a few.

UNITED STATES POLICY

The War on Drugs

Vast sums of money have been spent in the United States on combating illicit drugs. Strong moral condemnation and an equally strong commitment to jailing drug users have characterised the US policy positions. In 1972, Richard Nixon, who had, according to Davenport-Hines (2001, p. 338), developed a full-blown dependence on drugs by the time he was forced from office in 1974, was the first to declare a "war on drugs", unleashing a thirty-year war that has no end in sight. Nixon's and subsequent US presidents' war on drugs required "unconditional surrender from traffickers, dealers, addicts and occasional recreational users" (Davenport-Hines, 2001, p. *xii*). His predecessor Lyndon Johnson had declared a "war on poverty". Declaring war on somebody or something became a feature of post-World War II US presidents, with the possible exception of Jimmy Carter, although he did sanction covert actions.[3] Poverty, drugs,

---

[3] Carter's sole incursion into another country occurred in 1979 when he attempted to secure the release of United States hostages in Iran. Eight US soldiers were killed in the attempted release. Their subsequent release was secured on the day Carter's successor, Ronald Reagan, was inaugurated as President of the US. That their release should coincide with the first day of Reagan's presidency has raised serious questions about the circumstances in which the deal was done. The hostages were held for a total of 444 days. Many

Vietnam, Chile, Guatemala, Cambodia, Panama, Nicaragua, Grenada, Iraq — all have had war declared on them, officially or unofficially, by successive US presidents. Lee Anderson (1997), Hitchens (2001), TNI (2001) and Davenport-Hines (2001) detail recent US presidents' proclivity for war.

Dwight Eisenhower was directly complicit in the 1954 coup against President Jacobo Arbenz, the second legally elected president in Guatemalan history. John F. Kennedy sowed the seeds for full-scale war in Vietnam and only narrowly avoided nuclear war over the Cuban missile crisis. Richard Nixon's government was responsible for the overthrow of Chile's democratically elected president, Salvador Allende. His brief successor at the White House, Gerald Ford, continued Nixon's war on Cambodia. Jimmy Carter's administration supplied arms to the Mujaheddin in Afghanistan in 1979, who were at the time fighting the Soviets. These arms were paid for from the sale of opium and in the knowledge of the CIA. Ronald Reagan sought the overthrow of Nicaragua's democratically elected Sandinista government and bombed Libya in 1986 as a preventative measure against terrorist attacks. George Bush Sr declared war on Iraq in 1991 and Bill Clinton resorted to militarising Somalia's problems, cruise-missiled what he thought was a weapons factory in the Sudan but was actually nothing more than an aspirin factory, and also dropped cruise missiles on Afghanistan as a preventive measure against terrorism. George W. Bush declared war on Afghanistan and a more generalised war on terrorism in the aftermath of the attacks of 11 September 2001. His first two years have been dominated by war. In 2003, aided and abetted by British Prime Minister Tony Blair, Bush led his tautological "coalition of the willing" in a war against Iraq without having secured a United Nations mandate and in what many commentators believe was a breach of international law. The war mindset would appear to run deep in the psyche of US presidents and their administrations and is very much in evidence in their narcotics policies.

---

commentators have argued that Carter's failure to invade Iran and deliver the hostages during his tenure in office was one of the main reasons why he was not re-elected as president.

Richard Nixon, was the first president of the United States to declare a war on drugs and the first man in the White House to have "direct, calamitous influence on drug policy" (Davenport-Hines (2001, p. 338). Seven months after taking office in 1969, Nixon announced a global campaign against drugs and their traffickers. Nixon "saw evil Mexican traffickers exporting marijuana into the United States" (Rosenberger, 1996, p. 22) and he was determined at whatever cost to put a stop to them. He attempted to seal off the 2,500-long border between the United States and Mexico. He disrupted commerce and the movement of peoples across the border causing an "economic disaster for Mexico" (Rosenberger, 1996, p. 22). Mexican farmers and traders were held up at the border for hours on end as traffic was stopped and searched, causing their produce to rot in the hot sun. It had what Rosenberger calls "a chilling effect on US-Latin American relations (Rosenberger, 1996, p. 22). The net result of this initiative, according to Davenport-Hines (2001, p. 340), was that instead of importing its marijuana, the US became the world's largest marijuana-growing country.

Echoing Nixon's declaration of war on drugs, Ronald Reagan allocated over $1 billion to his first war on drugs in 1982 and his successor George Bush followed with a similar declaration and in addition mobilised the US army for the war. Federal spending on combating illicit drugs increased from $1.65 billion in 1982 to $17.7 billion in 1999 (Davenport-Hines, 2001, p. *xiii*). Bush Sr briefly reactivated Richard Nixon's 1969 short-lived two-week *Operation Intercept*. Bush too attempted to seal off the border with Mexico and block the supply of narcotics coming into the country in what became known as a "supply side" drug policy.

In addition to the supply-side approach, the US government adopted an uncompromising crime and punishment policy. Belligerent and bellicose attitudes and responses to drug production/dealing/use have characterised successive administrations in the United States since 1972, with, again, the possible exception of the administration of Jimmy Carter. A former head of the Los Angeles Police Department, Darryl Gates, suggested to the United States Senate Judiciary Committee in 1991 that recreational cannabis users "ought to be taken out and shot" (Walton, 2001, p. 140). Nothing really new in that suggestion, except for the absence of explicit racism. Bourgois (1995) states that during the cocaine hysteria of the early 1990s, "sheriffs in the deep South justified raising the calibre of their guns on the grounds that the cocaine nigger is sure hard to kill" (Bourgois, 1995, p. 278).

Of the $14.5 billion spent on combating drugs in 1996, 63 per cent was spent on law enforcement, 19.4 per cent on treatment and 13.6 per cent on prevention. By 1996, 300,000 of the 1.2 million prison population were incarcerated for drug-related offences at an additional cost of $20 billion a year (Klingemann and Hunt, 1998, p. 15). There are now more people in prison in the United States "than in any other democratic country at any time in history and more than half are there for drug-related crime" (Robson, 1994, p. 202). This punitive policy has little impact on drug production and/or consumption. Large-scale incarceration as a policy option has clearly failed.

In more recent times, William Bennett, who was appointed by George Bush in 1989 as Director of the Office of National Control Policy, a position that is popularly referred to in the US and in Britain as the "drug tsar", went so far as to suggest decapitation as a punishment for those who sold drugs to juveniles. He further argued that "drug enforcement officers should not be fettered by democratic views of legality and justice . . . declared that drug enforcement officers should be able to shoot down aircraft suspected of carrying traffickers" (Davenport-Hines, 2001, p. 361).

Reflecting general US policy of militarisation in international affairs as evidenced by the bombing of Iraq, Libya, Serbia, Sudan and Afghanistan, and its crusade against terrorism launched in the aftermath of the attacks of 11 September 2001, the United States has called on the military to help fight the war on drugs. In the densely murky world of international geopolitical jockeying for political/military advantage in the world, the policy of militarisation was clandestinely operating hand-in-glove with the covert use of drug trafficking with people like the Meo in Laos and the Contras in Nicaragua.

John Pilger (1998) claims that the CIA was "deeply involved in drugs: its secret army in Laos was run by General Vang Pao, the famous drug lord" (Pilger, 1998, p. 31), a view supported by McCoy (1991) and Davenport-Hines (2001). McCoy describes Vang Pao as "commander of the CIA's secret army in Laos" (1991, p. *viii*). Vang Pao was the commander of a 30,000-strong army of Hmong tribesmen formed to fight the communists in Laos, close to the border with Vietnam. The Hmong's main crop was opium and Vang Pao was allowed to use the CIA's Air America to collect and export the opium. In 1969, laboratories were opened to process the opium into heroin which was then transported to Vietnam and sold to US soldiers fighting the war there. After the Vietnam pullout, these laboratories sold directly to the United States, capturing, according to McCoy, one-third of the market in the United States.

Davenport-Hines (2001, p. 340) claims that arrests for marijuana consumption among US troops in Vietnam increased by a whopping 2,553 per cent between 1965 and 1967. When the US military sought to cut the supply of marijuana, the troops just switched to heroin. It was unreasonable, Davenport-Hines states, to expect soldiers to go into battle without some psychoactive substance to boost them. The experience in Vietnam did not dampen the enthusiasm of the CIA for covert operations involving trading in heroin. As noted above, during the Carter administration, cocaine profits were exploited by US officials to finance the Mujaheddin who fought Soviet troops in Afghanistan, a view again supported by McCoy. He claims that, in 1979, "the CIA covert warfare operation in Afghanistan provided the support for a major expansion of the southern Asia drug trade encompassing Iran, Afghanistan, Pakistan and northern India" (McCoy, 1991, p. 19). The objective was to cause general instability in the region but, in particular, it was aimed at destabilising the Soviet presence in Afghanistan.

Meanwhile, as Nancy Reagan was promoting a "Just Say No to Drugs" campaign, her husband Ronald Reagan's government was involved in efforts to depose the democratically elected government of Daniel Ortega, partially through drugs-funded covert operations. The congressional hearings conducted by Senator John Kerry (cited in Pilger, 1998, p. 31) concluded that "US policy makers were not immune to the idea that drug money was a perfect solution to the Contras — the forces opposed to the Sandinista government of Daniel Ortega". The chief investigator to the committee stated, "if you ask: in the process of fighting a war against the Sandinistas did people connected with the US government open channels which allowed drug traffickers to move drugs to the United States, the answer is yes" (Pilger, 1998, p. 31).

Chomsky (1989) claims that the United States foreign policy and its political elite remain dedicated to the rule of force. Chomsky claims that "violence and lawlessness frames their (US policy makers) self-image . . . troubled by some tactical disagreements over generally shared goals" (1989, p. 11). However, Chomsky claims that such policies are pursued without the consent of the electorate — one of the key issues of the Reagan presidency campaign was the fight against international terrorism. There was never a mandate for what followed. In the fight against terrorism, neither the electorate's consent nor the consent of global forums like the UN is regarded as necessary among the hawks of recent administrations. Violence and lawlessness also frames US policy on drugs. The "war on drugs" epitomises this policy. From Laos to Nicaragua, US drug policy has been determined by a political elite's preoccupation with the rule of force. The activities of Colonel Oliver North in the Iran-Contra Affair personifies this kind of duplicitous policy and practice.

Modern wars involving recent US presidents are feudal in nature, notwithstanding the use of sophisticated weaponry. Of late, feudal values have been replaced by the maxim of the Wild West. In the aftermath of 11 September 2001, George W. Bush invoked the spirit of the Wild West when he declared that Osama bin Laden was "wanted dead or alive". Bush Sr wanted Pablo Escobar, one of the most infamous drug-traffickers in Colombia, "dead or alive". If the current war on global terrorism fails to consider what threw up people like Osama bin Laden, it also fails to consider how Colombia came to be saddled with as notorious a person as Pablo Escobar.

The United States-led demand for cocaine came initially from its young professional class and later from the most marginalised and alienated people, from minority ethnic groups living in social, economic and ecological inner-city wastelands. Notwithstanding its illegal status, this demand for cocaine and crack (an alloy of cocaine and baking powder) proved to be a veritable goldmine for the more ruthless of the Colombian drug barons and Pablo Escobar was no slouch when it came to ruthlessness — nor for that matter were his adversaries — or to spotting an entrepreneurial opportunity. The entrepreneurial opportunity hit a major roadblock, however, when attitudes towards cocaine and crack within the United States hardened fundamentally.

The sea change in attitude emanated not as a result of the obvious devastation that was taking place in the inner cities but as a result of the death of University of Maryland basketball star Len Bias in 1986. The 22-year-old six-foot eight-inch Bias, who was being touted as an heir to the legendary Michael Jordan, collapsed and died as a result of snorting cocaine. His death and the public reaction marked a crucial turning point in the attitude to cocaine within the United States. In addition, the associated crime binge that many residents of inner city areas were forced to engage in to feed their habit was beginning to bite in the more affluent suburbs. In a society that had grown accustomed to good guy/bad guy scenarios, drugs and anybody associated with them became public enemy number one. Yet again it was time for all-out war. In April 1986, Ronald Reagan signed the National Security Decision Directive 221 declaring drug trafficking a threat to national security.

Crops, labs and traffickers in Central and South America were now fair game. The combined weight of the Departments of Defence and Justice were directed "to develop and implement any necessary modifications to applicable statutes, regulations, procedures and guidelines to enable US military forces to support counter-narcotics efforts" (National Security Archive, cited in Bowden, 2001, p. 73). For the hawks and adventurists within US federal agencies, the directive appeared to give them carte blanche for their more nefarious inclinations and yet another outlet for the US burgeoning arms industry.

Colombia is not the only South/Central American country that has experienced US militarisation. The avaricious appetite of the arms manufacturers continues to seek out new areas of deployment. In order to maximise their growth, they pump money into the political candidate who they believe will be most sympathetic to their financial well-being while continuing to fund the other party as an insurance policy in the event of them winning. And in President George W. Bush they have a willing accomplice. The Bush administration is firmly wedded to the growing militarisation of the war on drugs, the war on terrorism and the extension of US aerial and maritime control under the concept of hemispheric security (TNI, 2002).

According to the prestigious US *Mother Jones* magazine (April 2001, p. 47), arms manufacturers paid double the amount of money to the Republicans than they did to the Democrats. In what many interpret as a *quid pro quo*, the US government plans to increase military aid to Colombia ostensibly as part of its counter-narcotics strategy. *Plan Colombia* may have been the brainchild of a Democratic Party president but it has been enthusiastically incorporated into current Republican Party policy. *Plus ça change.*

The relationship between politicians and the arms industry does not end there. Carlyle is the eleventh largest US defence contractor (Shorrock, 2002, p. 26) and it has a virtual who's who of the Republican Party employed as consultants or advisors as well as former British Prime Minister John Major, former Thai premier Anand Panyarachun and former Philippine President Fidel Ramos. Former US Secretary of Defence and former deputy director of the CIA Frank Carlucci is the chair of Carlyle. Former President George Bush and former Treasury Secretary James Baker have, according to Shorrock, been hired "to exploit their experience in government and diplomacy to open doors and gather intelligence on investment opportunities" (2002, p. 26). The extensive overlap, both in terms of personnel and policy, between the two Bush administrations, would suggest that policy decisions by the younger Bush that result in increased militarisation may very well result in significant income for the older Bush and other senior Republican figures.

Now the campaign against drugs is not only militarised, but it is privatised as well. The privatisation of the war on drugs is now big business in the United States. According to a report by Julian Borger and Martin Hodgson in *The Guardian* newspaper (2 June 2001), a private corporation in Virginia called DynCorp carries out most of the aerial spraying of coca in Colombia. Another private company, AirScan, carries out aerial surveillance in Colombia. In such circumstances, corporate need and share-

holder values undoubtedly take precedence over the promotion of any real understanding of the drug issue.

While satisfying the domestic electorate, such policies do little for the peasants of the Andes who are the main producers of
coca, the plant from which cocaine is made and will do abso-
lutely nothing to quell the apparently insatiable Western-led
demand. Policies aimed at reducing or eliminating its production
fail to take into account its traditional, legal and cultural standing
amongst indigenous peoples in the region. Such policies are,
according to the Inter-American Indigenous Institute, "an attack
on the social, cultural and economic rights of the people and an
act of ethnocide and repression" (CIIR, 1991, p. 6).

War in Colombia

The overt criminalisation of drug production and the war
against drugs proved to be both a short-term godsend for
Escobar and other drug cartel leaders and a long-term night-
mare from which Colombia has not yet awoken. The current
cure, in the guise of *Plan Colombia*, is, many fear, as bad if not
worse than the original disease.

Bowden (2001) marks Colombia's decent into anarchy from
the death of Jorge Eliécer Gaitán in 1948. Gaitán was leader of
the Liberal Party, a lawyer and socialist described in a report
by the CIA "as a staunch antagonist of oligarchical rule" (Bowden, 2001, p. 13). He may have straddled the twin worlds of Colombian society — he was of mixed race and was visibly part of
Colombia's lower Indian caste — but he was educated and articulate, and to the governing elite he was a threat and an outsider. His assassin was himself murdered shortly afterwards
(much like the fate of another famous assassin fifteen years later
in Dallas, Texas). With the death of his assassin died the possibility of establishing the reason for his murder, but the finger of
suspicion was pointed at the CIA.

Life was hard in Colombia in 1948. For many Colombians,
Gaitán's death marked the end of any chance of breaking the
stranglehold of the oligarchs who owned and controlled the bulk
of Colombia's not insignificant natural resources. The powerful
US corporate sector provided these families, a privileged three

per cent who owned 97 per cent of Colombia's land and wealth, with the capital and technology needed to translate the oil, fruit, coffee and vegetables into much-needed foreign currency. With their new-found wealth, they not only built the beautiful boulevards of Bogotá but also enriched themselves. For the *campesinos* and the urban lower middle and working classes, their exclusion from their country's wealth seemed endless. Instead of having a slice of the wealth, the vast majority of Colombia's population had to contend with un(der)-employment, hunger and poverty. Their choices were limited, but from the 1970s onwards, the demand within the United States for an illegal white substance offered the possibility of unimaginable riches.

Colombia's coca was both plentiful and highly prized. As the demand for this product escalated in the 1970s, Pablo Escobar (1949–93), a relatively small-time crook from lower middle-class stock, headed the Medellín cartel along with the Ochoa brothers, Carlos Lehder and José Rodríguez Gacha. They and others were ready to cash in on this demand. Production flourished. The rewards were visible in Medellín and elsewhere. Escobar started his criminal life by stealing gravestones, sanding off the inscriptions and selling them on (Haskins, 2003). With the demise of the cocaine industry in Chile marked by the coming to power of the ruthless dictator, General Pinochet, production moved northwards to Colombia in what is referred to as the iron law of drug economics. Forced eradication in one area becomes the opportunity for another area to get into this very lucrative trade. Escobar was by this stage only too willing to take full advantage of this economic principle.

Drug trafficking in the 1970s became the largest industry in Colombia allowing the traffickers, according to Bowden (2001), to bankroll political candidates all the way to the president's office. Bank deposits in Colombia more than doubled between 1976 and 1980. By the mid-1980s, Escobar's personal property portfolio included

> nineteen residences in Medellín alone, each with a heliport, fleets of boats and planes, properties throughout the world, large swathes of land, apartment complexes, an international art collection, soccer clubs, a lavish country estate set

on a seventy-four-hundred-acre ranch, housing developments, and banks. (Bowden, 2001, pp. 29–36)

He was estimated to be the fifth richest man in the world at one
time — all from trafficking in drugs. Haskins (2003) estimates
that he was earning $500,000 a day at that time.

Unlike the wealth of the oligarchic families, the urban and
rural poor did not appear to resent this new-found wealth. By
growing coca, they too were beneficiaries, even if the trickle-
down was just that — a trickle. Escobar also appreciated the
value of patronage and benevolence. According to Haskins
(2003), in the 1980s, he personally financed the provision of
free medical and dental care to all the poor in Medellín, dis-
tributed 5,000 toys every Christmas to street children and
building a new Catholic church. He built five hundred homes
for the poor. His benevolence was not meant to go without notice — the development was called Barrio Pablo Escobar.

Not to be outdone of their share of this wondrous source of
wealth, establishment figures within Colombia began to claim
their stake. Accountants, politicians, lawyers, judges and the
whole range of the professional classes underpinned the enterprises of the narco-millionaires. By the end of 1986, a Colombian newspaper editor concluded that the drug cartels had
taken over Colombia.

The trade in illegal drugs was not, however, without its consequences. The drug cartel leaders' wealth was built on a reign
of terror, brutality, mass murder and a spiral of violence that
has lasted to the present day and has "knocked the entire country off balance and upended the rule of law" (Bowden, 2001, p.
30). The killings started early. In 1975, 40 people were killed in
an inter-cartel feud. By the mid-1980s, over 30 judges had been
killed. In 1985, the entire Supreme Court and its staff were held
hostage, resulting in 90 deaths. The mounting death toll was not
confined to Colombia. In January, the former Colombian Minister for Justice and then ambassador to Hungary was shot five
times in the face and killed.

Other high-profile deaths were to follow: the Attorney General Carlos Hoyos, presidential candidates Luis Galán and José
Antequera, leader of the Liberal Party and the Union Patriótica

Party respectively, and the Minister for Justice. After Galán's death in 1989, George Bush sanctioned $315 million for military, law reinforcement and intelligence to fight the Andean drug cartels, including $65 in military aid to Colombia. Yet the killing continued. In the first few months of 1991, there were on average 20 drug-related murders per day. Davenport-Hines (2001) claims that the military spend had the opposite effect to what was intended. Rather than crushing the Colombian cartels, as was the intention, they actually flourished. The cartels, rather than bowing to US military might, fought back. They "enforced their rules, and terrorised their opponents with pitiless violence, they corrupted politicians and officials and they contaminated the international financial system with laundered money" (Davenport-Hines, 2001, p. 340).

George Bush fingered Pablo Escobar as "the most wanted criminal in the world". Delta Force operators — Delta Force was the United States army's elite counter-terrorism unit — led by Colonel Jerry Boykin arrived in Bogotá in September 1992. With clearance from Bush, his Joint Chiefs of Staff Colin Powell and Defence Secretary Dick Cheney, he was instructed that they be given anything they wanted in pursuit of Escobar. The campaign against Escobar was directed by Morris Busby, the US ambassador to Colombia and, according to Joe Toft of the Drug Enforcement Agency, criminal gangs were active collaborators in the hunt. The killing of Escobar became the eventual goal, an end in itself. In 1993, Escobar was indeed assassinated.

The drug trade has taken a terrible toll on Colombia and the manner in which the deaths were executed is beyond the comprehension of most people. Fear pervaded Colombian society as the death toll mounted. From the genesis of Escobar's empire in the mid-1970s until his assassination, aided and abetted by the United States government, thousands of people were killed. His legacy was bloody beyond belief.

Yet Escobar's death did little to ease the convulsions that Colombia was experiencing. Colombia is now one of the most dangerous places in the world. In 2000, an estimated 35,000 people were killed (Abozaglo, 2001). Paramilitary groups, guerrilla units and the army kill and maim at random in the civil war and the drug war, which are intertwined, resulting in a culture of violence in the country. Reflecting on the role of the United States government in Colombia, *Economist.com* stated that it amounted to "bullying hypocrisy" (2001, p. 3).

Plan Colombia was presented by the Clinton administration as the panacea for Colombia's problems. The total cost of the plan was $1.319 billion. However, $162.3 million (12.4 per cent) of the budget was earmarked for US military and intelligence services; $116.5 million (8.8 per cent) was for upgrading US overseas Forward Operating Locations (see below); neighbouring countries were to receive $180 million (13.6 per cent); and Colombia was to receive $860.3 million (65.2 per cent).

Of this last figure, the bulk of the package, $519.2 million (60.4 per cent) was given to the military to secure southern Colombia, the traditional stronghold of the FARC movement, regarded by successive US administrations as guerrilla/terrorist organisation, and for drug eradication. The Colombian National Police received $123.1 million (14.3 per cent); alternative development was given $68.5 million (8.0 per cent); aid to the displaced were allocated $37.5 million (4.4 per cent); human rights $51.0 million (5.9 per cent); judicial reform $13.0 million (1.5 per cent); law enforcement / rule of law $45.0 million (5.2 per cent); and peace $3 million (0.3 per cent) (Centre for International Policy, 2003).

In reality, *Plan Colombia* simply added yet another layer of militarisation in its war against drugs on an already overly militarised country. Aerial bombardment and spraying chemicals on fields of coca with herbicides is central to the plan. (Clinton was not the first to introduce aerial bombardment. The first test-runs involving the spraying of herbicides on coca fields were conducted as far back as 1984.) A much more intensified round of spraying began in December 2000 despite strong opposition from local indigenous communities, civil society and from international organisations and bodies, including the European Union. *Economist.com* (2001) estimates that $440 million of American aid has been used to train three anti-drugs army battalions, totalling around 2,500 men and to equip them with sixteen Blackhawk helicopters.

Spears and Ó Loinsigh (2000) argue that *Plan Colombia* is seriously flawed because its primary target is the peasant producer and not the international narco-traffickers — many of whom live in North America and Western Europe — who retain 84 per cent of the value of the cocaine. Since December 2000, there have been significant increases in water contamination, deaths of domestic animals and skin ailments. Aerial fumigation has also caused serious damage to the Amazonian jungle. Producers are forced to move deeper and deeper into the jungle. As these croppers are followed by the herbicide attacks, the whole of the Amazonian eco-system is suffering from both ground and air assault. The use of *glyphosate* in the chemical mix, patented by the Monsanto Company, has added another layer of controversy to the fumigation process. Glyphosate has the effect of destroying the crop in a shorter time span. The long-term effects on the jungle and farming areas of Colombia are not yet known. The US is continuing to find new ways to eradicate more effectively. A new fungus, *fusarium oxysporum*, has been developed with "the goal to fumigate coca-growing areas thus intentionally creating an epidemic through biological warfare tactics making the Amazonian soil unfit for growing coca for many years" (TNI, 2002, p. 3).

In June 2001, the British chemical company ICI announced that it would no longer sell an additive, *Atplus 300f*, which was used in the chemical mix because it had not been tested for use in that context. Yet the Assistant Secretary of State for International Narcotics and Law Reinforcement Affairs claims that "no scientific evidence exists that eradication programmes damage human health" (TNI, 2001, p. 5) although he did admit to evidence of sanitation risks.

> The result of this programme is the eradication not just of the big plantations but also of the produce of small coca crop holders and alternative agricultural development projects, in the process putting at risk a much-needed local food supply.

Cassava, plantain, corn and other food crops have all been destroyed in the process, as have alternative development projects undertaken by a number of non-governmental agencies — all of which are vehemently opposed to the fumigation practices. As well as causing huge environmental damage, the fumigation process has also caused serious social upheaval, pushing the *campesinos* off their land as well as the *raspachines* — the temporary workers hired to harvest the coca leaf. Opposition to the policy of fumigation is growing. Klaus Nyholm, head of the United Nations International Drug Control programme (UNODCCP) has argued that "the fumigation of crops is not effective . . . I don't think you can spray your way out of this mess" (Jelsma, 2001, p. 7).

Meanwhile, neither the real profiteers from the drug trade — the heirs of Escobar, those who import and distribute it in the Northern Hemisphere — nor the increasing number of people involved in the production of illicit synthetic drugs, are affected by such policies and practices. And the political establishment will continue to insist that there is no other way. In this, as in other areas, the poor bear the brunt of such policies.

Given that the US takes a long view of what constitutes its backyard, *Plan Colombia* is no Mickey Mouse affair. It is, rather, a Trojan horse[4] within which US interests take precedence over local interests and considerations and in which covert activities can be undertaken in the guise of the war on drugs. It was, initially, as concerned with propping up support for former President Andreas Pastrana as it was concerned with the supply of drugs. Salvador Allende of Chile was the *bête noir* of the United States in the 1970s and Daniel Ortega of Nicaragua was in the 1980s. The FARC-EP, the Revolutionary Armed Forces of Colombian People's Army was, at the end of the last century, and continue to be, at the start of this century, one of the many irritants to US aggrandisement on the international scene. *Plan Colombia* is as concerned with ensuring that another Allende or Ortega will not emerge in Colombia as it is with eradicating coca.

Colombia is not unique amongst its South American neighbours. The militarisation of the anti-drug drive has increased US military funding in Nicaragua, El Salvador, Peru, Ecuador, Bolivia and Mexico. In these areas, new bases, called *Forward Operating Locations* (FOLs) have been established. Ostensibly, these locations are for fighting the war on drugs but

---

[4] I wish to acknowledge Jim Gleeson for the Mickey Mouse/Trojan Horse metaphor.

also conveniently provide a foothold in neighbouring countries, therefore enabling US military personnel to have a presence in these countries. Given the level of concern within the United States at the election of left-wingers Hugo Chavez in Venezuela (elected 1999), Luiz Da Silva in Brazil (elected 2003) and Lucio Gutiérrez in Ecuador (elected 2003), all of whom the current US administration view with deep-seated suspicion, military presence in other South American countries provides a surveillance platform against those they regard as hostile to their interests. Chomsky (2000) claims that this policy of locating US military personnel in South American countries was initiated by John F. Kennedy as part of US internal security and an anti-communist drive. Kennedy sent a military mission to Colombia in 1962 for this specific reason. The war on communism was Kennedy's Trojan horse. The war on drugs has replaced the war on communism as the modern day Trojan horse. It provides the rationale for US military presence in South America.

Efforts to dissuade and coerce people from cultivation of the crop have created divisions between families, villages and traditional leaders (van de Kook, 1993, p. 16). According to van de Kook, the production, commercialisation and consumption of coca is carried out according to age-old traditions which play a fundamental role in indigenous societies. The possibility of alternative livelihoods for poor peasant farmers involved in coca production is, according to the North American Congress on Latin America, "bleak, given 20 per cent urban unemployment and more than a million people internally displaced by violence" (North American Congress on Latin America, 2000, p. 56).

In addition, the obliterating slash-and-burn policies fail to take account of the importance of the coca leaf in the diet of these people: coca is a rich source of calories and other dietary elements. According to the Catholic Institute for International Relations (1991), coca includes protein, carbohydrates, calcium, phosphorus, iron, vitamin A and riboflavin as well as fibre" (1991, p. 1). In all, coca contains fourteen alkaloids, one of which is cocaine. According to Roger Cortez Hurtado (1993) — a Bolivian journalist and specialist on the politics of the drug trade — no one has satisfactorily explained the radically different reactions and behaviours of those who chew coca and those who consume its derivative cocaine. For Andean/Amazonian communities, coca is not cocaine.

Coca leaf also fulfils a very important social and spiritual function, a function that has been recognised by such world leaders as Fidel Castro, Queen Sofia of Spain and Pope John Paul II. These world figures publicly drank coca-leaf tea, *mate de coca*. Coca-leaf tea is a herbal drink that can help breathing at high altitudes. However, the principal use of coca is, as it has been for centuries, chewing. One farmer described its spiritual function as follows:

> We eat coca because in our culture, in our traditions, it is precisely the voice of coca, the spirit of the coca, which teaches us how to live well. It was as they ate coca that our forefathers were able to gather together and think and re-solve the problems of the world. For this reason they passed coca on to us that we should receive their wisdom (CIIR, 1991, p. 2).

The coca plant, *erythroxylum coca* and *E. novagranatense* is not only central to some of South America's precarious economies but it is also used to stave off hunger and fatigue as well as meeting traditional medicinal and ritual needs. Chewing coca leaves mixed with some alkaline ash

> releases an active compound [that aids] physical labour in the unforgiving heat of the tropical day, and it is also, like the synthetic amphetamine, a vasodilator, expanding the air sacs in the lungs and facilitating easy breathing in the rare-fied sky-high atmosphere in which these mountain commu-nities live. (Walton, 2001, pp. 104–5)

In order to meet these local and traditional demands, it is esti-mated that between 10,000 hectares in Bolivia and 12,000 hec-tares in Peru need to be produced. Slash and burn policies and aerial fumigation do not take into account these very important local considerations. Nor do these blunt tactics take into ac-count that the production of coca is, in many respects, the crop that keeps many countries from total economic disintegration and enables countries make repayments on the debts accumu-lated over the past 30 years. Financial institutions in the northern hemisphere like the International Monetary Fund and the World Bank may not like it publicly stated but the debt repayments they are so insistent on are only possible because of the production of the coca leaf.

Coca is very well suited to high altitude and a range of soil and climatic conditions. More than any other crop, it will thrive in a poor environment. Coca is also a high-yield crop, thereby suiting small or transitory landholders. Opium is similarly suited to such conditions. Were it not for the current construction of both opium and coca as the outcasts of all crop cultivation, aid and agricultural advisors would be to the forefront in encouraging their cultivation because of their suitability to both economic and physical conditions. Furthermore, coca production is rarely mono-cropped. It is not a stand-alone cash crop. It is produced in parallel with local food crops. Consequently, blanket bombardment of coca has the knock-on effect of killing off much-needed food supplies.

But in drug policy as elsewhere, the needs of traditional Andean and other societies take second place to the economic needs and political image-making of western policy makers. Efforts at diversification and crop substitution like the *Milka dairy* and the *Agroyungas coffee project* in the Los Yungas region of Bolivia have been both economically and ecologically unsustainable. The new coffee plants proved a total failure, as they were unsuited to the soil and climate of the area. According to the peasants and local NGOs, their unsuitability was compounded by inadequate technical advice. Having taken out credit to fund the project, the 1,500 peasants were then in debt and were threatened with the loss of their land (CIIR, 1994, p. 14). The Los Yungas experiment highlights the total inadequacy of one-dimensional approaches to development. Crop substitution has a role but it can only be effective when it is undertaken in conjunction with respect for human rights and indigenous culture and traditions.

This failed initiative highlights the importance of the way in which crop substitution is undertaken. The model, as opposed to the objective, was deficient. Crop substitution can only be effective when it is done incrementally, in consultation with local farmers, in a way that is compatible with the physical envi-

ronment and, most importantly, in a way that does not jeopard-
ise farmers' livelihoods, is respectful of social structures of local
communities and of their human rights. It also needs to be conducted within an overall development context that includes
health care, educational provision, sustainable employment
and welfare provision, amongst others, and within an overall
human rights framework. Crop substitution must eschew mono-
cropping. While maximised use of the land should be the target
to raise cattle, produce fruit or grain, plant trees or whatever
agricultural activity is most appropriate, all of this has to be
done in a way that is compatible with the environment and the
needs of the people.

Advocates of the sustained aerial bombardment of Colombia
claim that their methods have been vindicated by their results.
Coca production dropped in Colombia from 266,161 metric tons
in 2000 to 236,035 tons the following year — a drop of 11.3 per
cent or 30,126 metric tons. However, the net result of the fumigation was to push production into other areas. Production in Bolivia increased from 13,400 metric tons in 2000 to 20,200 metric
tons the following year — an increase of 6,800 tons or about 50
per cent. Production in Peru increased from 46,248 metric tons
in 2000 to 49,260 the following year an increase of 3,012 tons or
about 6.5 per cent (UNODCCP, 2002, p. 55).

Critics of *Plan Colombia* have not been confined to concerned individuals and the non-governmental organisations.
The European Parliament issued a resolution in February 2001
calling for necessary steps to be taken to "end the large scale
use of chemical herbicides and requested Colombia's President
Pastrana to stop environmental damage, contain the exodus of
internally placed inhabitants and stop fumigation" (TNI, 2001).

Paz Colombia, a broad-based platform of farmers, trade un-
ions, environmentalists, indigenous people and human rights
organisations, has called for measures that contribute to conflict
resolution and the de-escalation of war. In addition, they demand an end to the forced eradication of drug cultivation, the
decriminalisation of the small drug crop producer and the
involvement of affected communities in any alternative crop
production (Jelsma, 2001, p. 4). It is an indictment of the militarisation option and a flagrant abuse of military power. "More

militarisation, more guns, more police, more jails", argues Dr Roger Cortez Hurtado, have "just resulted in more people who take drugs and more criminal organisations" (1993, p. 6).

Notwithstanding the heavy-handed approach adopted by successive US administrations, there has been no demonstrable impact on the supply side and the number of people using drugs in the United States has continued to rise. Furthermore, the supply-side approach fails to take account of the growing use of synthetic drugs and the increase in production of nature-based drugs in the northern hemisphere. Rather than attend to domestic production, US policy focuses on the other, the foreigner, as the cause of its escalating drug consumption, and that becomes a justification for its covert war against its ideological opponents.

The drugs war is but one part of the new war that seeks to ring-fence the western "developed world" against the South, to portray the South as the new threat now that the old cold war bogey of the East has receded. Empires need enemies to fight and need to be constantly on the alert for war as much as they need friends and strong alliances. These enemies act as a kind of glue to bind its heterogeneous populations together and counterbalance its internal divisions. Prior to the events of 11 September 2001, and with the exception of Iraq, the United States was beginning to lack clearly identifiable enemies. The war on drugs filled that lacuna. The war on drugs conducted by the United States was not just perpetrated on countries of the South; it was also perpetrated against some of its own citizens. The unilateral no-drugs rhetoric was seriously undermined by the discovery that the US government had, without their consent, used illegal drugs on its own intelligence personnel. Walton claims that "irresponsible shocking dosages were given to people who had no idea what was happening to them, often over a period of days on end" (Walton, 2001, p. 120). Walton claims that the CIA was not only giving the drug orally but was injecting unsuspecting victims. Records received from the Gerald R. Ford Library, the former President of the United States, substantiate the allegations in at least one case, as the following reveals:

In the late 1940s, the CIA began to study the properties of certain behaviour-influencing drugs (such as LSD) and how such drugs might be put to intelligence use. On November 19, 1953, CIA personnel placed a dosage of LSD in drinks consumed by Dr Frank A. Olson a biochemist employee of the US army and other personnel. Prior to receiving the LSD, Dr Olson had participated in discussions where the testing of such substances on unsuspecting subjects was agreed in principle. (Memorandum for the President, 16 July 1975)

Dr Olson was not to know that he was the one to be experimented on, the chosen guinea pig. Shortly afterwards, he threw himself from the bedroom of his tenth floor hotel and died. On 12 October 1976, President Ford formally apologised for the behaviour of the CIA, stating that "an individual citizen should be protected from unreasonable transgression into his personal activities" (Ford, 1976). This one incident glaringly highlights the chasm between the US public and private policies and practices.

Within the United States, the war on drugs has had other serious budgetary implications. California incurred a $14 billion deficit in the 1980 because of its prison construction and maintenance programme. The prison spend resulted in fewer resources for areas of health, education, leisure and other programmes that may have gone some way to addressing the underlying structural inequalities. The most notable achievement, according to Bruce Bullington, has been "the wholesale incarceration of young men especially minority males at extraordinary rates" (1998, p. 126). The war has, he goes on to argue, been "calamitous in its results" (p. 128).

Reviewing US war on drugs strategy from across the Atlantic, Tim Murphy (1996) describes US policy not only as a political failure but as a racially prejudiced one as well. Apart from the obvious encroachment on civil liberties, it is, he argues "irresponsible in that it generates enormous and unjustified social costs" (1996, p. 52). But the concept of political failure as measured by Murphy may very well be a long way off the concept of political failure of first-term US presidents. For them, as for other politicians around the world, the only political failure that counts is not getting re-elected. If blanket-bombing of Colombian coca fields, causing social, economic and environmental upheaval, is what is required to secure re-election, then so be it.

The war on drugs serves other purposes: it often masks other wars. It provides pretence, an acceptable cover that will not only secure the public's compliance but also ensure public approval. The war on drugs was used as a justification for the war on terrorism long before the events of the 11 September 2001. The war on drugs also acts as a covert war on the poor, those in prison, on racial and ethnic minorities not just in the United States but elsewhere as well.

EU POLICY

Cannabis is the most commonly used drug within the EU, with at least 45 million (18 per cent) people having tried it at least once in their lives; up to 20 per cent of younger adults have tried it (EU Commission Report, 1999, p. 4). Amphetamine is the second most used illegal drug and it is estimated that its use is likely to be more significant in the future than ecstasy. Ecstasy is increasing in some member states but not in others. Heroin use appears constant but there is some evidence to suggest that a new generation of smokers is imminent. But the EU, like the US, is not just a consumer of illegal drugs; it is also a major producer, particularly of synthetic drugs.

The Commission report identifies the key drug-related "problems" as follows:

- The rise in the demand for drugs especially among young people;

- The increase in oral use of illicit drugs, such as ecstasy, new synthetic drugs and smoking heroin;

- The growing problem of the abuse of amphetamines;

- The frequent underrating of relevant health risks;

- The high prevalence of hepatitis C and HIV/AIDS as well as other serious diseases among intravenous users;

- The high number of drug-related deaths in many Member States (EU Commission, 1999, p. 14).

The Commission Report identified drugs as an ongoing threat to the population of the EU. Quoting from the results of the first Eurobarometer survey (1996) on drug use, the findings highlight that illicit drugs "considerably affect the life of the citizen" (1999, p. 6). On average, 14 per cent of the population of the EU has been in contact with "drug-related problems" of finding syringes in parks, seeing people openly dealing in drugs, and victimisation of violent crime (p. 6) over the previous twelve months. In addition, the survey reported "feelings of insecurity in European cities" (p. 6).

Whether such findings add anything of significance to our understanding is highly contestable. In terms of emotional impact, language like "considerably affect the life of the citizen", "drug-related problem" and "feelings of insecurity in European cities" has the potential to feed a sense of siege and unease, particularly among those living in the affluent suburbs. It could be equally argued that the fundamentally flawed design of cities, particularly the areas where poor and migrant people live, "considerably affect the life of the citizen". It is unlikely that such a finding will have the psychological impact that the conclusion that drugs "considerably" will have.

However, unlike policy in the United States where supply reduction gets most resources, EU policy is, arguably, more balanced with greater emphasis on demand reduction. While retaining a clear social focus, strong measures against users have steadily been put in place. The Commission Report to the European Council and the European Parliament locates the whole drug issue in its international context. The report states that

> the international dimension of the fight against drugs is widely recognised . . . and the emphasis has now shifted to . . . a broader set of human welfare issues addressing the social and economic dimensions of sustainable development in both producing and consuming countries. (1999, p. 6)

The Treaty of Amsterdam commits the EU to the development and implementation of policies that will have clear beneficial effects. Article 152(1) specifically stipulates "that Community action shall be directed towards improving public health, preventing human illness and diseases and obviating sources of danger to public health" (Treaty of Amsterdam, 1997, p. 246). In the Treaty, specific reference is made to "reducing drug-related health damage".

At its Helsinki meeting in December 1999, the European Council formally adopted the European Union Drugs Strategy (2000–2004). Six major objectives have been identified:

- To reduce significantly over five years the prevalence of illicit drug use, as well as new recruitment to it, particularly among young people under 18 years of age;

- To reduce substantially the incidence of drug-related health damage (such as HIV, hepatitis B and C, tuberculosis) and the number of drug-related deaths;

- To increase substantially the number of successfully treated addicts;

- To reduce substantially the amount of drug-related crime;

- To reduce substantially money-laundering and illicit trafficking in precursors (EU Commission, 1999).

Depenalisation — the tolerance of possession of small quantities of illegal drugs for personal use — has incrementally come to be accepted by many EU countries. A 1998 Belgian directive ruled that the possession of cannabis products for personal use should be accorded "the lowest priority" in criminal justice. (EMCDDA Annual Report, 2000, p. 24). Germany's policy provided a legal framework for injecting rooms; Switzerland has such facilities in place — a move the Irish government has resisted despite urgings to do so from Merchant's Quay Ireland and others. The consensus that drug users should not be imprisoned is gaining ground. A view is emerging that prisons are not appropriate places for drug addicts. Germany, Italy and Luxembourg have shifted policies from punitive measures to prevention and care.

BRITISH POLICY

Paradoxically, while the British Conservative Party was, at least up to the election of Ian Duncan Smith as its new leader, beginning to Europeanise its policies on drugs, the Labour Party in its first term in government appeared to move away from the European consensus. New Labour backed the "war on drugs" stance favoured in the United States. In a surprising move, a senior member of the British Conservative Party, Peter Lilley, called for the legalisation of cannabis and for it to be sold in government-approved outlets, a view that received cautious welcome from his colleague and one-time party leader pretender Michael Portillo. The flirtation with legalisation within the Conservative Party was short-lived.

New Labour's first-term policy of penalisation, moralisation, criminalisation, mandatory testing, new police powers and minimum sentencing was rooted in the moral panic of the 1980s. According to the Council of Europe Report *Social consequences of and responses to drug misuse in member states*, "the United Kingdom drug policy is based on the view that criminal sanctions are effective in deterring drug abuse and is primarily concerned with enforcement of the prohibition of certain substances" (Flynn, 2001, p. 7). The maximum sentences for all drug offences are amongst the severest in Europe.

In a series of three website broadcasts in February and March 2000, Tony Blair resorted to the war on drugs declarations. Not only had the content of New Labour policy become more reactionary but the tone became shriller. In the first of these broadcasts, Tony Blair declared:

> There's not a community, from here in the centre of London to the remote parts of our countryside, which is free from it (drugs). Not a parent — rich or poor — that doesn't worry. Not a family that is immune to the threat. (Blair, 18 February 2000)

The broadcasts reflect similar themes and reinforce the message delivered in the form of "A Personal Statement from the Prime Minister" in *Tackling Drugs to Build a Better Britain*. The time has come to "break once and for all the vicious cycle of drugs and crime, to continue the fight and come up with a truly imaginative solution" (Government of the United Kingdom, 1998). These combined statements on the effects of drug use cannot be dismissed as pre-election tactics or pre-election jitters, given what all the pre-election pollsters were predicting. Blair's "truly imaginative solution" implies that there is one elusive answer. His attempt to up the emotional ante, and whip up moral outrage at the prevalence of illicit drugs, places disproportionate emphasis on children and drug barons, the virtuous and the virulent (he is on the side of the virtuous).

This is not to gainsay the importance of highlighting the destructive influence of drug addiction but rather to highlight the narrow parameters within which Blair expostulates — or at least the way he did so in his first term — his drug policy. In addressing the destructive impact of drug use, he seems unable to go beyond the addiction paradigm. And he confines his moralising to the illicit drug trade.

Nor is there any recognition from Blair and others that drug supply is not just from the Southern Hemisphere, that there is a burgeoning drug supply industry in Europe and the United States as well. His complacency that the root cause of Britain's drug "problem" lies beyond its own borders is palpable:

> Those behind the evil trade don't recognise national borders. The drugs that cause the most damage to our young people and to our society are not grown here. They're often not refined here. Hard drugs sold on the streets of London or Glasgow (are) grown in Afghanistan or Colombia . . .
> (Blair, 10 March 2000)

In locating Britain's drug problem in countries like Afghanistan and Colombia without furthering any understanding of the macroeconomic circumstances that force these and other countries into large-scale export-oriented drug production and drug consumption, Blair risks feeding barely concealed xenophobic tendencies within a significant number of the British public. In addition, his contribution reinforces simplistic analysis and like his US counterpart the focus of his moralising is on the outsider, the other. He too is demonising, insinuating that the foreigner, the other, the stranger is contaminating the great British public. It is unlikely that Blair unintentionally singled out Colombia or Afghanistan for special mention. He too is jockeying for geopolitical advantage, albeit on the coat-tails of the United States.

Not only do these underlying values drive Blair's internal policy, but he is also bringing pressure on EU accession countries to adopt similar approaches. In calling for support for these countries to fight against international crime and drugs, he offers increased assistance in training police and customs officers and extra resources for sniffer-dogs to detect the drugs and computer software to detect money laundering from the sale of these illicit drugs.

Two further developments highlight Blair's approach to the drug issue. The UK Criminal Justice and Court Services Bill published in March 2001 proposed drug-testing offenders at every stage of the criminal process and withdrawing the passport of anyone convicted of a drug offence. On 9 April 2001, Blair announced a £300 million boost to tackle "the evil of drugs in Britain", £220 million (73 per cent) of which is to be spent over three years "for police and local communities in England and Wales to disrupt local drug markets and drug-related crime" (Blair, 2001).

Blair's zeal "to win" the war on drugs was matched by his first anti-drug co-ordinator (drug tsar), Keith Hellawell. For Hellawell, everyone coming into the country was to be regarded as a potential drug smuggler. The former police chief constable proposed testing tickets of air travellers for drug residue.

Reviewing New Labour's first term drug policy, Professor Gerry Stimson, in a trenchant criticism of the Blair approach, described the policies as "punitive and coercive" ones that "stigmatise, marginalise and stereotype" (Stimson, 2000, p. 1). The Council of Europe Report, *Social Consequences of and Responses to Drug Misuse in Member States*, in 2001 stated that "the government of the United Kingdom . . . continue(s) to place great emphasis on attempting to deter drug use by means of severe legal penalties, despite evidence that this approach lacks utility" (McDermott, 2001, p. 2). The policies "demonise and overly criminalise the drug user and mark a re-orientation away from a health focus". Agreeing with Stimson's analysis, McDermott sees British drug policy in this period as "being driven by a rigid puritanical ideology that looks to the USA for solutions to the UK's drug policy" (2001, p. 1).

Politicians' own behaviour, however, often belie their bellicose anti-drug rhetoric. While Thatcher was vowing in 1989 to "take firm action" against "crack peddlers" who would "find no safe haven" in Britain (Davenport-Hines, 2001, p. 362), at least two of her cabinet colleagues were planning a night of drug-taking. Alan Clarke recalls in his diaries (Davenport, 2001, p. 388) how his colleague Nicholas Soames — described by BBC News (2003) as a "constitutionally conservative politician" — regaled him in the chamber of the House of Commons one day about "an incredibly powerful new aphrodisiac" he had discovered. Both men subsequently retired to Soames's flat where he brought down a phial.

Such behaviour may very well explain Conservative Party double-think on illicit drugs, the rhetoric for public consumption and experimentation for private consumption. Stimson (2000, p. 1) states that the Conservative Party era was marked by "a pragmatic public health approach to issues of sexual behaviour and injecting drug use". In Stimson's view, the 1987–1997 policy era was based on helping problem drug users to lead healthier lives and to limit the damage they might cause to themselves and others. Many of these pragmatic user-centred policies remain. What has changed is the general atmosphere in which local policies are being implemented.

In New Labour's second term in office, two fundamental changes took place in British drug policy. The war on drugs was now linked to a greater war — the war to protect civilisation and all civilised people from fundamentalists and evil terrorists who seek to destroy western civilisation and democracy. Blair was quick to point to the war on drugs as a justification for the war on terrorism in Afghanistan, notwithstanding the massive drop in production levels as a result of the Taliban edict. As is his wont, the pitch both in terms of content and tone was emotional. The war against the Taliban, fought in conjunction with the Northern Alliance in Afghanistan, was presented as a war to protect British youth:

> The arms the Taliban are buying today are paid for with the lives of young British people buying their drugs on British streets. That is another part of the regime that we should seek to destroy (TNI, 2001, p. 2)

"We will bomb their poppy fields", declared the Prime Minister. Without furthering any evidence for his charge, Blair went on to declare that Osama bin Laden and the Taliban had "jointly exploited the drugs trade" and warned Britons to be prepared for "a new invasion of Al Qaeda opium" (TNI, 2001, p. 2). Blair either refused to acknowledge that since the Taliban imposed their July 2000 ban on opium production there were very few fields left to bomb or else he was being deliberately mischievous. No subsequent evidence emerged of the predicted invasion of Al Qaeda opium.

Blair saw the linking of drugs to the "war on terrorism" as a way of justifying Britain's involvement in what many in that country saw as a US war. It was a ruse designed to feed the moral panic that exists about drugs and justify the loss of innocent Afghani life. The sub-text was that these lives are not so innocent after all, that in fact that they are the cause of the premature deaths of so many British people. In shifting the blame for these deaths on to the shoulders of peasant farmers in Afghanistan, Blair was also avoiding any accusation of the complicity of his government's and that of previous governments' policies in the death of "young British people".

The second change in second term New Labour policies was the new Home Secretary David Blunkett's announcement to the Home Affairs Select Committee that he was proposing to reclassify cannabis from a Class B to a Class C drug. Calling for "an honest and common sense approach", Blunkett stated that "there was a clear need to focus more effectively on hard drugs that cause the most harm and to get people into treatment" (Blunkett, 2001). However, the Home Secretary did emphasise that re-classification was not to be confused with (re)legalisation. Cannabis is to remain a controlled drug and using it a criminal offence with a maximum penalty of two years for possession and five years for supply. Reclassifying cannabis as a Class C drug means that "offenders" can now be dealt with on the spot by police and warned, cautioned or reported for summons. There is currently no power of arrest for Class C drugs.

In addition to this major policy change, David Blunkett announced that, subject to the satisfactory outcome of clinical trials, he would approve changes in the law. These changes would enable the prescription of cannabis-based medicine, that he would examine prescribing heroin for patients in carefully controlled circumstances and that he was not averse to providing safe areas for injecting heroin users.

These announcements, given New Labour's initial policies and the pronouncements of the Prime Minister, were unexpected. They were made against a background of a policy that hitherto been constructed on penalisation, moralisation and criminalisation. However, Blunkett was careful not to distance himself too much from the previous policy framework. He stressed the ongoing need to warn young people that all drugs, including cannabis, are dangerous. Lest the announcements be interpreted as a softening on overall policy, the press release detailing the proposed changes were headed "Blunkett to Focus on the Menace of Hard Drugs".

In formally announcing the change in the reclassification of cannabis from a class B to a class C drug in the British House of Commons in July 2002, Blunkett was careful to ensure that this policy change was not going to be interpreted as "going soft on drugs". The old rhetoric was still there about "the misery caused by drug abuse" and the change in the reclassification was matched with a ringing declaration that "we will increase the sentences for trafficking and dealing in class B and C drugs to fourteen years'" (Blunkett, 2002).

Oliver Letwin MP, the Conservative Party Shadow Secretary of State for the Home Department, in response to the Home Secretary's announcement described it as an attempt to "wrong-foot all his opponents, buying off the libertarians with increasing liberalisation, and the anti-drugs lobby with a show of toughness" (Letwin, 2002).

Blunkett estimated that the current cost of drug use in Britain exceeded £10 billion. Keith Hellawell suggested not more than four years earlier that the cost was £4 billion, suggesting either that there was a massive rise in the intervening years or that such estimations are not exactly a precise science. To what extent the announcement in the House of Commons will effect significant change in the lives of those most intimately affected by the use of drugs remains to be seen.

DUTCH POLICY

At the other end of the continuum lies Dutch policy. Long regarded as liberal, if not permissive, in its tolerance of drugs compared to that outlined above, its approach reflects a different value system. According to Dutch Drug Policy Fact Sheets published by the Netherlands Institute of Mental Health and Addiction, the main aim of Dutch drug policy is to "protect the health of individual users, the people around them and society as a whole" (2001, p. 1). Priority is given to vulnerable groups and to young people in particular.

The Netherlands has chosen a less absolutist position than either the US or Britain in its drug policy, notwithstanding changes introduced in 2002. The distinction between soft and hard drugs is, according to Derks et al. (1998, p. 81), "the cornerstone of Dutch policy". The Opium Act (1976) distinguishes between hard drugs like heroin, cocaine and ecstasy — which the Dutch government regards as posing an unacceptable health risk — and soft drugs like cannabis which are regarded as low-risk. Their policy, unlike that of the US or indeed of New Labour in Britain, is not dominated by moral overtones, nor does Dutch policy share the same punitive approach. The sale of small quantities for drugs for one's own personal use is openly tolerated, and possession of small quantities has, in effect, been decriminalised. Recognising that criminal law on its own can never be an effective response to illicit substance use, Dutch policy favours manageability over prohibition.

Dutch policy reflects the expediency principle. "People are going to use drugs anyway; so let's try and restrict it somehow" is one way of describing this principle. Dutch "coffee houses" allow the sale of soft drugs for personal consumption but they are not allowed to advertise and no hard drugs can be sold. They must not be a nuisance to their neighbours and they cannot sell to young people. Sales of drugs cannot exceed five grams. Notwithstanding such easy availability, Flynn (2001) reports that "intensive cannabis use in The Netherlands is extremely rare" (Flynn, 2001, p. 17). Despite this, there would appear to be some change in attitude to these coffee houses, while recent times have witnessed tighter regulation of coffee houses. Since the beginning of 2000, there has been a drop of 11 per cent in the number of coffee houses, which has coincided with the decentralisation of regulatory powers to local municipalities and also reflects growing international pressure on the Dutch government to reign in its tolerant policies.

In adopting this position, the Dutch government is attempting to prevent drug users from entering the illegal environment where they are difficult to reach, or from having to purchase from criminal drug dealers. Since 1998, the Dutch authorities have also experimented with the prescription of heroin under strict medical supervision. The experiment involves a group of 750 serious users whose physical and mental condition is poor and who are unable to function properly in society and whom the government considers cannot be helped by the regular care system. In addition, the Dutch government provides methadone — 12,500 of the 28,000 opiate addicts are on methadone (Flynn, 2001, p. 9) — clean needles, food, medical care, accommodation, assistance in managing finance and in finding work. Accordingly, Dutch drug policy is subjected to much international attention and, as outlined above, no little disapproval.

If, by international standards, The Netherlands has adopted a tolerant policy, it still retains a strong preventative policy. According to Spruit (1999, p. 107) the Dutch government "sets a high value upon primary prevention within schools". The main aim is to delay or postpone for as long as possible "inevitable adolescent experimentation by means of credible information". In addition to offering factual information, national school prevention programmes also promote behavioural skills such as teaching young people to deal with peer pressure and improving independent decision-making. The avoidance of exaggeration and sensationalism are key elements of their education programmes. Alcohol and drugs, according to Spruit (1999, p. 108), "have been stripped of their taboos and sensational images that previously acted as an attraction".

Following the presentation of the Flynn Report, *Social Consequences of and Responses to Drug Misuse in Member States*, in draft form to the Joint Oireachtas Committee on European Affairs, on Wednesday 8 November 2000, *The Irish Times*, the following day, reported that the Netherlands had "spectacularly impressive results" in controlling the safe use of drugs. In comparison to the UK, the Netherlands had lower levels of cannabis use despite its public availability and fewer drug-related deaths. The estimated prevalence of problem drug use amongst the general population (aged 15–54) in the Netherlands is 3/1,000 whereas the corresponding figure for the UK, where there is a much stronger punitive approach, is 6.6/1,000 (Flynn, 2001, pp. 13–14). While using the term "problem drug use", the Flynn Report bemoans the fact that "there are no rigorously defined and generally accepted criteria (Flynn, 2001, p.4) for measuring problem drug use.

Non-problematised use is also lower in the Netherlands compared to the UK and this holds true across a range of different illicit drugs. Twenty-five per cent of the UK population aged between 16 and 59 have used cannabis at some stage in their lives whereas just over 20 per cent of Dutch people have used cannabis. Three per cent of the UK population have used cocaine, ten per cent have used amphetamines, four per cent have used ecstasy and one per cent have used heroin. In the Netherlands, just under three per cent have used cocaine, just over two per cent have used amphetamines, two-and-a-half per cent have used ecstasy and less than one per cent have used heroin. The figures for the 16–24 age group show even lower consumption rates in the Netherlands compared to the UK (Flynn, 2001, p. 16).

While comparability of current data is an inexact science, with particular difficulty attached to precise understandings of "drug-related deaths", indications are that drug-related mortality in the Netherlands is lower than elsewhere. There were 2.4 drug-related deaths per million in the Netherlands in 1995, compared to 9.5 in France, 20 in Germany, 23.5 in Sweden, and 27.1 in Spain. Compared to the UK (England and Wales only), the Netherlands has had a consistently lower mortality rate. Not only that, the death rate in the Netherlands has remained relatively stable, whereas the death rate in the UK has climbed considerably. In 1986, the drug-related death rate per million of the population was 2.6 compared to 25.8 for England and Wales. By 1999, the death rate in the England and Wales had almost doubled to 49.9 per million, whereas the death rate in the Netherlands had only increased by 1.2 per million to 3.8 per million (Flynn, 2001, p.18). The Netherlands Institute of Mental Health and Addiction in its *Fact Sheet* states that Dutch mortality figures are the lowest in Europe. The death rate from illicit drugs in the Netherlands is significantly lower compared to the death rate from alcohol — estimated at 2,000 per year — and tobacco — estimated at about 20,000 per year (Flynn, 2001, p. 19).

The debate on Dutch drug policy is similar in many respects to the debate on abortion. Not only have the Dutch eschewed the criminalisation of abortion but abortion is openly available and is not subject to the same taboo as it is, for example, in Ireland. The Dutch also claim that they have the lowest abortion levels of any other country in Europe — a claim that is strongly contested by those who oppose abortion. Legalisation of abortion, they claim, has resulted in lower levels of abortion — tolerance of "soft drugs", they claim, has resulted in the lowest drug-related mortality in Europe.

IRISH POLICY

Irish drug policy is very much more in keeping with EU policy and is markedly different from British policy in a number of respects. The language of the policy as outlined in the National Drugs Strategy 2001–2008 is more discursive and less judgemental compared to, for example, the statements of British Premier Tony Blair as outlined above. While this country was no stranger to substance abuse in the past, drug use came upon an unsuspecting public, catching policy-makers and service providers unawares. Murphy-Lawless (2002) dates the arrival of heroin into the north inner city of Dublin to the spring of 1981; Butler (2002) dates its arrival to 1979/80, while the Garda Commissioner claims that heroin was introduced into Dublin in 1969 by small-time criminal groups (Byrne, 2001, p. 3).

"Drug abuse" is defined in official government literature as:

> the use of any drug, legal or illegal, which damages some aspect of the user's life — whether it is their mental or physical health, their relationships with their family, friends or society in general or their vocational functioning as stu-

dents or as workers inside and outside the home (Health
Promotion Unit, Department of Health [no year given] p. 2).

Irish drug policy in the mid-1970s — at least as reflected in Dáil
debates — was characterised by a more languid, complacent
attitude to drug use when compared with what was to come in
the following decade. Former Health Minister John O'Connell
argued in 1977 from the backbenches, while a member of the
Labour Party, that cannabis could not be presumed to be a
dangerous drug, claiming that "it was no more dangerous than
a glass of beer" (Butler, 2002, p. 128). O'Connell was unknow-
ingly anticipating Noel Gallagher's "cup of tea" analogy.
Charles Haughey, the then opposition Fianna Fáil spokesperson, argued for the necessity to differentiate between "hard"
and "soft" drugs during the 1977 debate on the Misuse of Drugs
Bill, introduced by the Tánaiste and Minister for Health Brendan
Corish. Haughey also expressed concern about the effects of
the Bill on civil liberties and "wondered about the credibility of
anti-drug legislation in a society which was so tolerant of alcohol and tobacco" (Butler, 2002, p. 128). Reflecting on the debate that had taken place in both houses of the Oireachtas, the
then Senator Michael D. Higgins stated that the debate in the
houses was markedly different from the debate that was taking
place outside the Dáil and Seanad. Public discussion, he argued
is "often insensitive and crude" (Butler, 2002, p. 129) unlike
what he regarded happened in the course of the debate of the
Misuse of Drugs Bill, which finally became law in 1977.

Michael D. Higgins's assessment might have been accurate
in 1977 but by 1984, when the next Misuse of Drugs Bill was being debated, attitudes had hardened. Outside of the Oireachtas,
attitudes were less forgiving than what one might glean from the
1977 debates. While attitudes towards alcoholics and the person
"who enjoyed a few jars" was quite indulgent, attitudes towards
those that either experimented with or were addicted to drugs
was less benign. Experimentation with drugs was perceived as
evidence of human frailty and the result of individual foibles.
Scant regard was given the social, familial or environmental or
structural factors that contribute to drug use.

The findings of the Working Party on Drug Abuse 1968–1971, which was established by Health Minister Seán Flanagan, reflected this individualistic perspective while downplaying the extent of drug use in the country. There were, however, a number of far-seeing recommendations. Reviewing the findings of the Working Party from a distance of 30 years, Butler (2002) describes them as "well argued . . . clearly presented . . . moderate . . . carefully considered, balanced evenly between treatment and prevention" (Butler, 2002, p. 112). The Working Party argued that increased police powers should not curb individual freedoms and that a distinction should be made between personal possession and possession for the purpose of sale or supply. The Working Party argued that penalties should reflect the kind of drug involved and that cannabis should be treated more leniently than other drugs.

However, despite these and other recommendations and despite the passing of the Misuse of Drugs Act 1977, the decade of the 1970s left this country singularly unprepared for what was to come in the following decade. The early 1980s "were characterised by a poorly prepared official response" (Morgan, 2001, p. 10). The lackadaisical attitude that prevailed in the 1970s was quickly replaced by moral panic, a panic that resulted in politicians resorting to the war on drugs rhetoric. By 1982, Health Minister Michael Woods threw down the following gauntlet:

> The government has declared war on drug abuse. We are determined to attack and root out this new cancer which is eating into our community. Although we were sheltered from the waves of harmful drugs that flooded Europe in the last decade, we are no longer exempt from their insidious influence. (Butler, 2002, p. 164)

Woods's tenure in Health was short-lived due to the fall of the minority government of which he was a minister. During his second tenure, he commissioned the Bradshaw Report at the request of local TD Tony Gregory and local Catholic priest Paul Lavalle in September 1982, a report that according to Butler (2002) focused on the unpropitious social and environmental factors that are strong predictors of drug use. The Bradshaw Report, which did not receive the unqualified support of all inner-city community activists and residents, nevertheless confirmed what people already knew from locally based sources. The Dublin north inner-city study concluded that "there was a ten per cent prevalence rate of heroin use in the 15–24 age group for the year prior to survey, while the rate was twelve per cent for the 15–19 age group and for girls in the 15–19 age group it was thirteen per cent" (Butler, 2002, p. 139). The study also concluded that the Mountjoy A electoral area had a prevalence of heroin use "that was comparable with, and in some cases worse than, some of the more notorious drug ghettos in the United States" (Butler, 2002, p. 140).

Woods' second brief tenure in Health coincided with what became known as the Gregory deal. Tony Gregory was and still is (in 2003) an independent TD for Dublin Central, a constituency that includes Mountjoy A electoral area. In what was at the time viewed as an audacious move, Gregory agreed to support the minority government if it implemented a number of specific social and economic measures that would address the rapid growth in heroin addiction in inner-city Dublin and the attendant urban neglect and consequent decay. Garret Fitzgerald (1991, p. 404) estimated the cost of these measures at £150 million, of which £82 million would be spent in 1982. The historian and academic Dermot Keogh (1994, p. 360) estimated the deal at £50 million while Barry Desmond estimated that the deal would cost between £60 and £80 million (Desmond, 2000, p. 66). Tony Gregory has subsequently estimated the potential cost of these measures as in excess of £200 million with the housing content alone at more that £50 million.

Fitzgerald later stated that the deal "astonished everyone, and horrified many" and dismissed the demands as "a long list of goodies" (1991, p. 404). Not "everyone" concurred with Fitzgerald's analysis. Historian and academic Joe Lee argued that

> what was disgraceful . . . was less the deal than the fact that it needed a deal to win some attention for one of the most deprived areas of the country, an inner city constituency ravaged by poverty and neglect, and their concomitants, unemployment, bad housing and a vicious drug problem. (Lee, 1989, p. 508)

Barry Desmond of the Labour Party replaced Woods and was Minister for Health and Social Welfare from November 1982 to March 1987. He established a Special Government Task Force on Drug Abuse in 1993. Yet, this Task Force seems not to have registered very highly on the agenda of at least three members of that administration. This period of government from 1992–1987 is unusual in that Barry Desmond, one of the ministers, and the Taoiseach in that administration have written their memoirs and another minister, Gemma Hussey, published a diary of her tenure in government.

Despite the fact that the Task Force consisted of six ministers of state under the chairmanship of Fergus O'Brien, Minister of State at the Department of Health and Social Welfare, it does not appear to have made any impact at cabinet level. Garret Fitzgerald makes no reference to it in his account of his tenure as Taoiseach during this period. The only reference that Fitzgerald makes to the escalating heroin epidemic in his whole autobiography is during a special two-day cabinet meeting in Barrettstown Castle in the summer of 1993, when he states that "we also discussed the drug problem". He does not state what conclusions they reached or actions they planned. That reference is the sum of what Fitzgerald has to say in his autobiography about the growing heroin epidemic, one of the biggest social scandals in the capital city.

Gemma Hussey makes no reference to the discussion of the drug problem at all, preferring to limit her observations to the landscape outside the window of Barrettstown Castle. She informs the reader that they were "surrounded by long windows where one can see the rolling lawns and meadows, horses and trees . . ." — a long way from the ravaged communities of inner-city Dublin (Hussey, 1990, p. 47).

That administration did introduce the Misuse of Drugs Act 1984. Now politicians were less likely to discriminate between serious and debilitating drug use and recreational drug use. A minority of politicians called for a heavy-handed approach. In a Dáil debate in 1984, Fine Gael TD Brendan McGahon called for "extreme measures" to be taken — echoing the views expressed by the former LA police chief mentioned earlier. He made uncritical reference to policies in other countries where "drug pushers are dealt with summarily by being shot" (Butler, 2002, p. 144) while not actually advocating that position. Fellow TD Hugh Byrne, echoing xenophobic views on the cause of drug use, claimed in the Dáil that "all of Dublin's drug problems had their origin amongst foreign students at Trinity College Dublin" (Butler, 2002, p. 128). Such views were not confined to the Dáil chamber. Independent Dublin City Councillor Joe Connolly suggested that the army be called in to take drug addicts off the streets. Drug addicts were "Jekyll and Hyde characters who become evil at night when they get drugs" (Butler, 2002, p. 198), he declared.

The Misuse of Drugs Act 1984 reflected the change in tone of the debates and adopted a more punitive approach. Penalties were increased, the mandatory requirement that judges should defer sentencing until they had received medical and social reports was dropped, and it became an offence to print or publish, any book, periodical or other publication which either advocates or encourages the use of any controlled drug. In this respect, the 1984 Act was very much in line with US and British thinking. Drug use was the result of individual as opposed to a societal or environmental failure. The remedy was sanction-based. Rather than addressing the social, educational, environmental and financial issues that drive consumption in marginalised communities, the 1984 Act concentrated its attention on supply as opposed to demand reduction.

Of the two ministerial accounts and the account of the Taoiseach that exist from the period 1982–1987 there is hardly a mention of the changing drug landscape in this country. Such was the level of attention that working-class communities whose quality of life was being seriously eroded were getting from their national government.

The 1980s were marked by tug-of-war power struggles with communities affected by the heroin epidemic on the one side and health officials and health professionals on the other. This tug-of-war story is well told in both Butler's (2002) and Murphy-Lawless's (2002) accounts. The officials sought to assert the primacy of professional judgement and institutionalised response while community activists asserted the primacy of their knowledge of their own needs and that of their communities.

Locally based groups and individuals were very strong in their convictions that only they could fully understand the impact of heroin addiction on their communities. Though they might assert that they were well qualified to be involved in programmes that would counter the epidemic, they were beholden to state officials for resources to undertake this work. Those living in drug-affected communities eschewed the individualism that characterised official drug responses and instead sought a broad-based co-ordinated response that would address not just individuals' needs but the holistic needs of marginalised communities. Inner-city communities and their spokespersons consistently argued for a social and economic response that would address the underlying causes of serious and life-threatening drug addiction. The frustration of those communities with the official response to the crisis in their communities was palpable.

The change of government in 1987 did not bring about any real change of policy. New Health Minister Rory O'Hanlon's innate conservatism was very much in evidence when it came to making decisions that would address a key emerging issue in the drugs debate, namely the spread of HIV/AIDS infection. An indication of O'Hanlon's position on drug policy emerged in the course of a Seanad debate in 1998. John O'Connell, now a member of Fianna Fáil and who was to succeed O'Hanlon as Minister for Health, was calling for methadone maintenance programmes and free needle provision to counteract the spread of HIV/AIDS. Apart from saying that he was monitoring the international situation, O'Hanlon demurred. In a subsequent speech in the same year, O'Hanlon reported on his review of international practice, claiming that there was "insufficient evidence to support the introduction of free condoms or needle exchange for drug users" (Butler, 2002, p. 184).

Nonetheless, such practices were already quite established, highlighting the disjunction between official policy and actual practice, a situation according to Butler (2002) which was not very unusual. Harm reduction strategies/goals such as needle exchange, methadone maintenance and condom use, were being advocated by state agencies like the Eastern Health Board and the National Drug Advisory and Treatment Centre at Jervis

Street Hospital; furthermore, such organisations were also facilitating drug users in accessing these facilities.

Such harm reduction strategies/goals were to receive the official imprimatur in 1994 with the publication of *Shaping a Healthier Future: A Strategy for Effective Healthcare in* the 1990s during the tenure of Brendan Howlin of the Labour Party as Minister for Health. While less than one page of the 75-page document is given over to addressing drug use, key policy changes are flagged in the document. As well as addressing supply issues, the strategy recognises the need for addressing demand issues:

> It is accepted internationally that to deal effectively with the problem of drug misuse, a strategy must be in place, which encompasses measures to tackle both the supply of and demand for illicit drugs. (Department of Health, 1994, p. 61)

The strategy identifies seven strategies/goals to combat drug misuse built around prevention, treatment and rehabilitation services. Most notably, the proposals include reference to harm reduction, a significant break with previous government policy. The document states that "harm reduction and assessment services will be provided to drug misusers" (Department of Health, 1994, p. 61)

The policy of harm reduction was further underlined in the *Second Report of the Ministerial Task Force on Measures to Reduce the Demand for Drugs* (1997). In the Chairman's Foreword, Democratic Left Minister for State at the Department of Enterprise, Trade and Employment, Pat Rabbitte, declared that "we have developed a strong philosophy of harm reduction" (1997, p. 6). Recognising that in the past the state neglected to address the underlying forces of economic and social marginalisation, there was now an acknowledgement that there was no single answer to the problem.

Prevention rather than reliance on treatment and rehabilitation afterwards was the strategy adopted by the 1997 Task Force, with education, information and the development of youth and sport facilities as the three main planks of the prevention strategy.

The minority Fianna Fáil–Progressive Democrat government that was elected in 1997 was the first government to appoint a Minister of State with responsibility for drugs. Chris Flood was appointed Minister of State at the Department of Tourism and Trade with special responsibility for Local Development and the National Drugs Strategy. However, that government's economic policies were seen by many as exacerbating the structural inequalities that contribute to crippling drug use. They were also the first government in the history of the state to oversee a booming economy and to be in a position to make real choices on social distribution.

The Combat Poverty Agency (CPA), the State agency established in 1986 to work for the prevention and elimination of poverty and social exclusion, in its 1998 Report warned that "a booming economy does not guarantee an end to poverty and an inclusive and just society" (1998, p. 3). The Report went on to say that the better-off and those at work have gained disproportionately from the economic boom. Ongoing concern has been expressed about the allocation of resources, none more so than with the coalition's first budget. In the 1997 budget, two-and-a-half times the available budget was spent on tax cuts than were on social welfare increases. Income differentials increased and redistribution policies were inequitable in this and subsequent budgets. The Report further itemised deficiencies in core public services, the poor position of children in Irish society, with one in four living in poverty, and ongoing educational disadvantage.

CORI, the Conference of Religious in Ireland, was more scathing in its analysis of policies to address social exclusion. In a press release dated 6 June 2001, CORI described the government's plan to address social exclusion and poverty as "an insult to poor people". The Report went on to "indicate [their] deep disappointment at the government's failure to provide clear targets for the elimination of poverty". CORI argued that "the poorest people in Irish society are being left further and further behind and the gap between them and the rest of society is widening dramatically. . .". CORI's analysis is supported by the Economic and Social Research Institute (ESRI). A report published by the Institute states that during the 1997–2002

FF/PD government, "the top 60 per cent of earners gained substantially, while the lower 40 per cent gained below the average" (Brennock, 2003). Ireland is not unique in this respect. The
social engineering that passes for globalisation is increasing
the disparity between rich and poor. Aart Scholte (2000, p. 215)
claims that, globally, "when governments are faced with a
choice between sustaining social policy and improving global
competitiveness, governments tend to favour the latter". This
neo-liberalism is a new form of social engineering and Ireland
provides a classic example.

While the economic policies of the current and previous
governments have attracted their fair share of criticism, their
rhetoric in relation to inclusion has been faultless. Current drug
policy is a case in point. In his speech to launch the National
Drugs Strategy, the Taoiseach Bertie Ahern stated that "communities remain at the heart of any serious effort to tackle
drugs" (2001). Community-based initiatives along with agencies like health, education, housing, estate management, employment, recreation, sport and policing and involving local
communities in the development and delivery of locally based
strategies are identified in the reports as the way forward. Central to the Irish approach has been "the bringing together of
key agencies in a planned and co-ordinated manner, to develop a range of appropriate responses . . ." (Department of
Tourism, Sport and Recreation, 2001, p. 94).

Confirming drug policy location within a social exclusion
framework, the Taoiseach, at the Drugs Strategy launch, committed the government to funding and implementing the strategy "in the context of overall social inclusion policy". This is in
keeping with commitments entered into under the Programme
for Prosperity and Fairness where drug policy is detailed in the
section dealing with social exclusion (2000, p. 82). Likewise, the
National Development Plan locates drug policy within a social
exclusion framework. In acknowledging that "not everyone has
benefited proportionately from this new-found prosperity", the
Plan states that "many marginalised areas are disproportionately affected by . . . drug abuse [and consequently] suffer from
poorer health and lower educational achievement resulting in
lower employability". The Plan goes on to say that alleviating

poverty and building an inclusive society will yield "multiple benefits" (2000, p. 37). Regrettably, the economic policies required to effect serious change has not matched the rhetoric.

To his credit, the Taoiseach did not single out any particular ethnic group as the cause of Ireland's drug-related difficulties. His speech was free from the xenophobic undertones that have characterised the speeches of some of his international counterparts. His stance was noticeably different from that of his British counterpart and his language was measured and optimistic, even if he appeared to operate from a "havoc" paradigm.

Four key elements underpin this strategy, which have evolved over the past three years around "four distinct but inter-linked pillars" (Department of Tourism, Sport and Recreation, 2001, p. 50):

- Supply reduction

- Prevention, including education and awareness

- Treatment, including rehabilitation and risk reduction

- Research.

While the actual term "harm reduction" is not included in the overall strategic objective of the National Drug Strategy 2001–2008, harm reduction is at the core of the strategy. The overall strategic objective is as follows:

> To significantly reduce the harm caused to individuals and society by the misuse of drugs through a concerted focus on supply reduction, prevention, treatment and research. (Department of Tourism, Sport and Recreation, 2001, p. 4)

In naming these four key elements, the government recognises that "there is no single universally acceptable effective response model" (2001, p. 94). Nor can the drug issue be addressed in any meaningful way by one agency. Locally based, planned and co-ordinated community-based interventions are central to the strategy. This involves voluntary groups working in partnership with statutory agencies on education, awareness, prevention treatment and rehabilitation. The Local Drugs Task

Forces retain their key role in developing policies and responses within broad agreed guidelines.

In what may yet be regarded as an unprecedented approach, government policy is actively decentralised.[5] Fourteen Local Drugs Task Forces — North Inner City, South Inner City, Ballyfermot, Ballymun, Blanchardstown, Clondalkin, Coolock, Crumlin, Finglas/Cabra, Tallaght, Cork City, Bray, Canal Communities, and Dun Laoghaire/Rathdown — have been established by the government. Each includes representatives from local community and voluntary groups as well as statutory agencies. Approximately 220 projects (Ruddle et al., 2000, p. 20) received funding through the LDTF initiative. These agencies work collaboratively in responding to the drug problem in their area. The bulk of the work undertaken by these projects was in the area of education and prevention (51 per cent) followed by treatment and rehabilitation (36 per cent), education and prevention and treatment and rehabilitation (7 per cent), supply/control (3 per cent) and research and information (3 per cent) (Ruddle et al., 2000, p. 27).

To this end, the government in 1997 made available £30 million for a Young People's Facilities and Services Fund (YPFSF) over three years to support a variety of capital and non-capital projects in disadvantaged areas. The primary focus of the fund as outlined in the National Drugs Strategy 2001–2008 is on LDTF areas and selected urban areas of Galway, Limerick, South Cork City, Waterford and Carlow. Under the National Development Plan (2000–2006), £102 million has been provided for this fund (2001, p. 56). Over 340 projects are being developed as part of the YPFSF.

Taken together, the recommendations of the First and Second Task Forces and the National Drugs Strategy 2001–2008 show a greater emphasis on involvement of community groups in the development and implementation of drug policies.

---

[5] There is some conflation or confusion in public policy debates about the terms decentralisation and deconcentration. Decentralisation involves decision-making at local level. Deconcentration involves the administrative location of a centralised executive in the regions while maintaining control at the centre.

In January 2001, a Drug Court was established with a view to enabling drug users who come to the attention of the courts to undergo supervised and rehabilitative processes rather than enter into the criminal system. Crime reduction is its primary focus. These Courts do not, however, eschew the punitive model: the Court does not exclude punishment "should the circumstances so warrant" (National Drugs Strategy 2001–2008, p. 58).

Despite all the rhetoric, however, the Irish strategy does retain a strong punitive dimension. Shaken by the death of *Sunday Independent* crime correspondent Veronica Guerin, the Irish State responded with a raft of legislation that caused concern to many civil liberties activists. The Criminal Justice (Drug Trafficking) Act (1996) allowed for the detention of a person suspected of drug trafficking for up to seven days. The Criminal Assets Bureau Act (1996) resulted in the establishment of the Criminal Assets Bureau. The Proceeds of Crime Act (1996) and the Disclosure of Certain Information for Taxation and Other Purposes Act (1996) allowed for the exchange of information between the Revenue Commission and the Gardaí. These were followed by the Bail Act (1997), which allows for the refusal of bail to a person who has been charged with a "serious offence". The Housing Act (1997) allows for the exclusion of person(s) from local authority houses who are judged to have engaged in antisocial behaviour.

While the death of Veronica Guerin might have been the catalyst for the introduction of the above legislation, concern had been mounting about the effect that heroin use was having, particularly on working-class communities in Dublin. The First Report of the Ministerial Task Force on Measures to Reduce the Demand for Drugs (1996) estimated the number of heroin users in the greater Dublin area at 8,000. In December 2000, there were 5,032 people on methadone maintenance compared to 4,332 at the end of 1999. In the combined Health Board areas, 6,043 were receiving treatment for drug use in 1998. Murphy-Lawless (2002) puts the most recent (1999) estimates of opiate drug use in the greater Dublin area at 13,460 (2002, p. 14).

These statistics disguise the sheer awfulness of heroin addiction, the human wastefulness, not only for the user, but for the immediate and extended family and for whole neighbourhoods, in the case of Dublin, which was and continues to be disproportionately affected by heroin. Current Irish policy recognises this. In introducing the National Drugs Strategy 2001–2008, the Minister with responsibility for the National Drugs Strategy, Eoin Ryan, who replaced Chris Flood as the responsible minister, wrote as follows: "Drug misuse is one of the great social ills of our time. It affects individuals, families and whole communities." He was, however, optimistic about the potential impact of the policies outlined above. Through the implementations of the recommendations outlined in the Strategy, this country can, he writes, "turn the tide on one of the greatest threats facing our young people and society" (2001, p. 4). Whether this strategy is capable of turning the tide remains to be seen.

The evidence from the evaluation (this author was one of the evaluators) of Local Drugs Task Force projects suggests that progress is being made. The evaluation consisted of face-to-face interviews with managers of 142 projects. It concluded that

> despite the difficulties and pitfalls . . . the majority of projects perceive that they are succeeding in implementing what they have set out to do. (Ruddle et al., 2000, p. 97)

Over 68 per cent of the project managers believed the original objectives have been reached "to a great extent" and the remainder (32 per cent) are confident their objectives have been attained "to some extent" (Ruddle et al., 2000, p. 72).

Despite the legislation, the reports, the studies and the activism, drug use continues to pose a major social policy challenge. To adopt a phrase that has become current in another contested issue in this country: they have not gone away.

THE LEGALISATION/(RE)LEGALISATION/ DECRIMINALISATION DEBATE

One way of ending the war on drugs is to (re)legalise all illicit drugs and simultaneously introduce tight controls on the sale and distribution of all drugs. That, at least, is the argument put forward by a growing number of activists, academics, politicians and people working in the field. However, of all the policy issues within drugs, the debate on (re)legalisation is possibly the most contested. Even the language used is contested. Legalisation allows for the sale of drugs in certain controlled circumstances. Decriminalisation would involve the removal of existing legislative restrictions on the sale, distribution and consumption of drugs and replacing them with controlled and restricted outlets for their sale and consumption. (Re)legalisation highlights that drugs were once legal and as a result of various policy decisions are now illegal. Given that this reflects the historical reality, the term (re)legalisation will be used except in quotations for the rest of this section.

While there is growing demands from both activists and academics (Walton, 2001; Robson, 1994; South, 1999; Murphy, 1996; Bourgois, 1995; Davenport-Hines, 2001) for the (re)legalisation of drugs, their demands are strongly resisted by governments across the world. Their demands have not found favour with the general public either. Officially, the consensus is holding: illicit drugs, including cannabis, are perceived as bad and dangerous and (re)legalisation would be the equivalent of throwing petrol on the fire. In this country, only 24 per cent of respondents in Bryan et al.'s study stated that cannabis, the drug that is perceived to be least harmful, should be (re)legalised (2000, p. 33). The debate on the (re)legalisation of drugs has been constructed and conducted from polar opposites.

If the nineteenth century was characterised by a tolerant attitude to drugs, the twentieth century was characterised by control. The first control on the sale of drugs was introduced into Britain in 1868 with the Pharmacy Act. Walton (2001) and Mott and Bean (1998) cite exaggerated newspaper reports as the reason for the introduction of the Defence of the Realm Act, 1916. Reports were emerging that prostitutes were plying soldiers on leave from the front with cocaine in the West End of London with the concomitant risk of undermining the war effort. Britain's security was not going to be put in jeopardy by a combination of prostitutes and drugs. The Dangerous Drugs Act was introduced in 1920 and it prohibited the production, importation, exportation, possession, sale or distribution of opium, cocaine, morphine or heroin except by persons licensed by the

Home Secretary. Further legislation was introduced into Britain in 1923, 1925, 1932, 1964, 1971 and 1985.

The impact of such a raft of legislation is, as outlined above, highly contested. Those who oppose such legislation and want to return to nineteenth-century conditions argue that the whole enterprise has been an unmitigated disaster. In attempting to criminalise drugs, governments have, according to Walton, "landed themselves with the most baleful disaster in legislative history" (2001, p. 95). A transnational criminal class has been created with dire consequences for both illegal and non-illegal drug users. Bourgois (1995) claims that there is one simple, cheap and effective way to disarm this violent criminal class and that is to destroy their profits by decriminalising drugs. As well as having beneficial effects on the consumer, Bourgois also argues that this would have beneficial effects on the producer as the whole panoply of measures that are currently being used to reduce the supply would no longer be required.

The truth is, according to Robson, that tens of thousands of people in Britain (and elsewhere) are faced with the challenge of raising £100 or so every day of their lives to maintain their supply of heroin or cocaine (1994, p. vii). That figure has since grown exponentially. Tim Murphy, one of the most vocal proponents of (re)legalisation in this country, sets out his stall as follows:

> I regard prohibition as ineffectual, irresponsible, and illegitimate. It is ineffectual because it is falling far short of its objectives, it is irresponsible because it is contributing directly and indirectly to the creation of greater social problems and it is illegitimate because it employs incarceration and other criminal sanctions in an improper and excessive manner. (Murphy, 1996, p. 33)

Underpinning such views is the belief that the desire for intoxication is universal and all the legislation in the world will not frustrate attempts to fulfil that desire. The desire for psychoactive substances is embedded in human consciousness and evidence of that desire dates back to antiquity. Such a desire is acknowledged by the continued legality of alcohol and tobacco, two drugs that many commentators believe to be much more harmful than many of the proscribed drugs.

The call for (re)legalisation is presented as a call to reality and for common sense to prevail. Laws require consensus and the advocates of (re)legalisation believe that no consensus exists on the current prohibition. Instead, double standards and double-think prevail in what Walton describes as "a twilight zone of begrudging tolerance" (2001, p. 95).

Those who support a change in the current policy of prohibition received a major fillip towards the end of December 2002 when 100 members of the European Parliament, including Irish member Patricia McKenna of the Green Party, signed a Proposal for Recommendation calling for the reform of the conventions on drugs. They describe the current position as a failure:

> the long history of prohibition has clearly demonstrated that relying mainly on action taken by the State through criminal law and the police has only a marginal effect in controlling the abuse of narcotics and psychotropic substances. Despite massive deployment of police and other resources production and consumption of, and trafficking in, prohibited substances have increased exponentially over the past 30 years, representing what can only be described as a failure. (European Parliament, 2002, p. 3)

The parliamentarians called for the reclassification of substances and the legalisation of the use of drugs "for purposes other than medical or scientific ones" (European Parliament, 2002, p. 4).

The supporters of the current prohibition counter-argue, in the words of Tim Rathbone, former Chairman of the All Party Drug Misuse Group of the House of Commons and cited in Robson, that "arguments for legalisation are born of despair" (Robson, 1994, p. 200).

James Q. Wilson was appointed Chairman of the National Advisory Council for Drug Abuse Prevention by President Richard Nixon and remains one of the most outspoken opponents of the call for (re)legalisation. Legalisation would, he argues, "very likely remove the stigma attached to habits that are damaging to not only the physical health but also moral personality" (Wilson,

1994, p. 360). Acknowledging the high cost of the current policy, those that argue in favour of the status quo do so in the belief that the cost of (re)legalisation would be even greater. It would require an unprecedented shift in policy, social engineering on a scale not attempted in any other area. Such social engineering is, they argue, just too risky. It would let the genie out of the bottle and it is not, they believe, a kindly genie.

Echoing Wilson's view and citing experimentation in Switzerland that allowed the sale of drugs in a restricted area, Garda Commissioner Pat Byrne argues strongly against any moves to change current practice, with the possible exception of allowing the use of cannabis in restricted and controlled medical circumstances. The Commissioner succinctly outlined his objections to (re)legalisation as follows:

> Decriminalisation would increase risks and costs to individuals, families and communities — indeed every part of the nation — without compensating benefits. Greater availability of drugs would lead to greater use and more overall problems associated with drugs. Society would have to contend with more traffic accidents and more industrial accidents due to impaired judgement; more educational failures; more homelessness; more destroyed careers, and families, domestic violence; more AIDS and more babies born addicted. (Byrne, 2001, p. 8)

While the National Drugs Strategy 2001–2008 does not address these issues, it clearly endorses the views expressed by Commissioner Byrne. The Review Group believe that "the *present* [my emphasis] provides a *solid foundation* [their emphasis] from which all those involved in trying to tackle the problem should work for the future" (National Drugs Strategy 2001–2008, p. 95).

SUMMARY

This chapter has outlined broad policy parameters within which drug policies are formulated. The British-US axis would appear to be built on a shared ideological base, adapting a more offensive, belligerent stance focusing on the supply side and talking hard and, in the case of the US, acting hard against producers, particularly in Colombia, though not apparently in Afghanistan.

The "war on drugs" has become inextricably linked to the "war on terrorism". In that environment, the blunt instrument of aerial bombardment and the privatisation of drug control finds a ready acceptance amongst the ever-declining number of people who vote at election time. Notwithstanding such policies, there is a body of historical evidence that suggests that agents of the US government have engaged in and worked with drug traffickers in order to advance their own self-interests. Covert operations have been put in place to fund, in the case of Nicaragua, insurgency and, in the case of Colombia, counterinsurgency activities. All of these were conducted while officially advocating a "say no to drugs" policy.

In contrast, EU policy, with the possible exception of Great Britain (although recent policy developments would suggest that Britain is coming more into line with the general thrust of European policy), is more focused on demand reduction and on implementing policies that will mitigate the worst excess of drug-related problems at both individual and community level. However, there are policy variations within the EU, with countries like the Netherlands to the fore in adopting what are regarded as more tolerant if not expedient policies. While allowing for variations between member states and with the exception of the United Kingdom, Irish policy is very much within the EU mainstream while retaining a strong punitive attitude towards drug trafficking and also in some cases to minor drug offences.

Irish policy has undergone major change in the last three decades. Initially governments were slow to recognise and respond to the growing threat posed by drug use. In so far as they did respond, their focus, in keeping with what was happening internationally, was on supply reduction and the pathologising of individual drug users. Equally, government and their agents were suspicious of community engagement as a way of addressing the needs of those most affected by the epidemic of heroin addiction that hit in the early 1980s and continues to impact today. Now policies have evolved to the extent that local engagement is seen as the best way of addressing the insidious impact of serious drug use. Equally, initial policies focused on the individual have given way to more holistic policies that recognise that for interventions to be effective they must encompass a whole range of socio-economic interventions. Effectively, if not overtly, government policy now recognises that drug use is here to stay, and that while prevention and prohibition will always remain a policy goal, the more pragmatic goal of harm reduction has become part of official government policy. Reflecting on Irish drug policy, O'Brien and Moran (1997, p. 28) have identified a significant shift from the aspiration of creating a drug-free society to the current policy of harm reduction.

The discussion has also highlighted the way in which drug consumption is unresponsive to legal sanction. There would even appear to be an inverse relationship, at least when comparing Great Britain with the Netherlands, between the level of consumption in a country and the severity of the measures to discourage consumption. Britain has adopted a more punitive approach but has a higher level of consumption, whereas the Netherlands has adopted a less punitive approach and has a lower level of consumption. This chapter has attempted to summarise the polarised positions adopted by the pro and anti (re)legalisation lobbies.

In conclusion, it is difficult to isolate the extremely lucrative global drug trade from the murky geopolitical power struggle within which it operates. Some politicians seek to present the fight against drugs as the struggle between western civilisation and fundamentalists seeking to destroy it; between the forces of good and evil; the virtuous and the virulent; the forces of darkness versus the forces of light; the good guys and the bad guys. The reality is that such neat dualisms do not exist in the world of *realpolitik*. Yet that is how the international trade is often presented. Naming and labelling is a powerful way of controlling how one perceives situations. That applies in particular to the drug trade. In order to understand the global phenomenon of the drug trade, it is necessary to go beyond such facades. The reality is that within the international arena the corrupting influence of drug trade, even on the good and the virtuous, cannot be underestimated.

Chapter 3

DRUG USERS: PERCEPTIONS AND REALITY

INTRODUCTION

Understanding difference is a key to understanding drug use. Drugs users are heterogeneous people and their needs, like those of the rest of the world's population, are not amenable to simplistic classification and response. Just as people are very different despite social and cultural similarities, so too are drug users. This chapter will review some of the key issues that have emerged from a review of the literature in this area.

Invariably, the discussion on drug use is always situated in the context of the use being problematic. Problematisation of drug use by the general public appears to be confined to a limited number of drugs and to a certain cohort of the population. Yet every drug has risks. Chetley (1995) claims that "no drug can be devised which, whether given to women or to men, and whether used by the oral, nasal, retinal, cutaneous, subcutaneous, rectal or vaginal route will be totally free of all risks" (1995, p. 1). Alcohol, cigarettes and over-the-counter (OTC) drugs, as well as the huge array of prescribed drugs, are as potentially problematic. However, these drugs are not problematised in the same way as are, for example, cannabis, heroin and ecstasy. Cannabis is regarded as less problematic than heroin, ecstasy and cocaine.

Bloor and Wood (1998, p. 9) challenge us with the assertion that "defining drug use as a problem demands attention to the sociological question: a problem for whom?" Certainly the HIV/

AIDS scare of the 1980s and latterly the concern about hepatitis brought more focus to this debate as the link between intravenous users and HIV/AIDS and hepatitis became well established. Clearly, intravenous drug users who contract HIV/AIDS and hepatitis require a response from the health services.

In so far as funding for drug use comes from the proceeds of crime, then it is a problem for the policing and judicial systems as well as for the broader community. As some communities are overcome by destructive drug consumption, it becomes a problem for estate managers and community leaders. But more fundamentally it becomes a problem for many of the residents in these local communities, and particularly problematic for children who may be exposed to drug-related activities, syringes and other drug paraphernalia.

Clearly, for those whose drug use is life-threatening or life-reducing or harmful, either to their physical or mental health and well-being, or to the physical and mental health of those close to them, quite rightly their use has been problematised. There are also huge social and economic costs attached to serious drug use, both in terms of real costs and opportunity costs, which is a problem for the whole of society. There are unquantifiable costs and problems for the individuals and families who have experienced dysfunctional behaviour, addiction, bereavement or imprisonment, or have contracted infectious diseases, and where chaos and despair have dominated their lives and those of their families and communities. There are costs too for people who have never or only occasionally used drugs but who have been affected by drug-related crime.

However, not all drug consumption can be characterised as such. Important variables come into play in differentiating between people's drug use. There is a significant difference between the occasional recreational user and the addicted user. Equally, there are significant differences in female and male consumption patterns. Other variables that affect the nature of consumption include living in a rural or urban area, being in prison or out of prison, sexual orientation, membership of the dominant ethnic group or a member of a minority group, social class — all of these impinge on people's overall experience of drugs. In defining and problematising drug use, therefore, it is necessary to differentiate between users rather than adopt an approach that views all users as a homogenous group.

This chapter examines this and other questions:

- How are drug users perceived by non-drug users?

- Are there specific differences in the way women and men experience drug use?

- What is the typical age profile of the drug user?

- Are social class, ethnicity and race predictors of drug use?

- Is sexual orientation any predictor of drug use?

- Can prisons effect change in a person's drug consumption?

- In what way do environmental factors contribute to drug use?

PERCEPTIONS OF DRUG USERS

Conflicting images emerge as to what constitutes a typical user or the degree to which one can actually profile a user. The stereotype, however, as in all stereotypes, is much easier to profile. He — and in the stereotype it is invariably a he — comes from a dysfunctional family in an urban working-class area. Regarded as feckless and shifty, he has failed in school, as opposed to the school failing him, is thought to be of low intelligence, amoral, with no religious attachment, irrational, easily led and both emotionally and verbally inarticulate.

Seeking short-term gratification, his judgement is perceived to be clouded from lack of discipline, short-sightedness and preoccupation with the self. Butler (2002) claims that drug users are often regarded as "self-evidently pathological and deviant . . . were assumed to demonstrate high levels of psychopathology (Butler, 2002, pp. 176–7). The response from many who do not have direct contacts with users has been, in the words of former British Prime Minister John Major in a different context, to understand less and punish more. These comments were directed at the killers of two-year-old Jamie Bulger — a view, as we have seen, that his successor has inherited.

The reality, according to some commentators, is different. McCoy et al. (1996, p. *xv*) claim that the great majority of users are not psychologically disturbed and assert that much of their use is simply part of adolescent activity and an affirmation of their own identity, signifying their moving on from the world of their childhood. Experimentation with drugs and alcohol marks, for many young people, a rite of passage to the adult world where substance use is, if not endemic, at least widespread. For some commentators these rites of passage reflect a robust and confident approach to life as opposed to those who approach life in a timid and fearful way. Morgan et al. (1996) cite a study by Shelder and Block (1990) that suggests that "adolescents who had engaged in some drug experimentation — primarily with marijuana — were the 'best' adjusted of the sample", whereas adolescents who, by age 18, had never experimented with any drugs "were relatively anxious, emotionally constricted and lacking in social skills" (Morgan et al., 1996, p. 23). Korf and Buning (2000) and Riley and O'Hare (2000) reflect a similar perspective on young people who are currently experimenting with a range of substances. Just like anyone else, they argue, "most drug users want to survive and make the best of their lives" (Korf and Buning, 2000, p. 129).

Howard Parker (1998, p. 160) argues that drug users apply a cost–benefit analysis to their drug use. Each drug is routinely discussed for its uppers and downers, effects and side-effects and users make what they regard as informed decisions on their use. According to Parker, the "assessment formulae took in immediate health risks, the implications of discovery, particularly by family or employers, the cost of the drugs as against other consumption options (e.g. alcohol), the after-effects of the drug in mood and performance and the propensity of the drug to provide relaxation, energy, a buzz etc.". Parker takes a very optimistic view of young people's decision-making ability. He argues that young people are clear about their limits and that their drug taking is a rational choice with the aim of producing or inducing pleasure.

Plant and Plant (1992, p. 7) agree, arguing that "most users are not stupid". There is, they argue, "nothing inherently deviant or abnormal in the use of psychoactive drugs". Most people who use drugs do so because the effects are enjoyable or rewarding in some way. They argue that most drug use is recreational. Just as older people live in a "wet" culture where drinking is both widely practised and generally regarded as a legitimate and enjoyable practice, so too younger people live in a "wet" culture but also participate in a "powder" culture that is also part of many older people's world.

Harrison and Pottieger (1996, p. 13) argues that young people are very discerning when it comes to deciding which drug to use. The choices made, she argues, are not random, a view that is not shared by Murphy-Lawless (2002). She claims that

> many young people are prepared to experiment widely with illegal drug use, that they are prepared to take chances over the issue of the quality of the street drugs they buy and they are prepared to mix cocktails almost indiscriminately. (2002, p. 14)

Carlen and Morgan (1999, p. 163) conclude that taking drugs is a calculated risk decision to "produce or induce good times in a fast moving uncertain world".

Robson (1994) and Walton (2001) oppose basing assumptions of the typical drug user on "the highly non-representational problem drug user" (1994, p. 9) while Walton (2001) argues that the "addiction paradigm" (p. 78) has resulted in the punitive approach to drug use. Robson (1994) argues that cannabis-using adolescents are more likely to be left-of-centre in their political world view, have more tolerant attitudes towards minorities like gay and lesbian people and ethnic minorities. Such tolerant views have in fact been presented as evidence of the corruptibility of drugs. In a pamphlet published in 1998, a Utah State University professor is quoted in Walton (2001, p. 15) as having claimed that the drug-addicted teenager may display "an excessive preoccupation with social causes, race relations and environmental issues". While trying to avoid stereotyping, Robson (1994, p. 8) states that "the typical drug user is likely to posses at least some of the following characteristics: rebelliousness, non-conformity to conventional values, a tolerant attitude towards unusual or deviant behaviour, a relative lack of interest in schoolwork or in having a career, early sexual experiences, independent and single-minded with a reluctance to abide by the rules". Non-conformity to church, mosque, synagogue or temple and to the state and a defiance of social control would appear to characterise the typical drug user in so far as one can generalise. Concomitantly, he also believes that at least some have impaired emotional intelligence and low-self esteem. Robson (1994) also claims that US research indicates that early experimentation in drugs come from families who have a history of active participation in political protest groups. Children from conventional families are more likely, he argues "to produce children with an in-built resistance to deviating from the norm and less inclined to buck the system" (1994, p. 10).

However, drug use is not just a by-product of anti-establishmentarianism. Drug use is also high among aspiring professionals, both here and abroad. Claims of use within this section of the population made during the public consultation process leading up to the publication of the National Drugs Strategy 2001–2008, and by the European Monitoring Centre for Drugs and Drug Addiction (EMCDDA), would seem to lend credence to this view. A study of 1,000 students conducted in 1998 by the Union of Students in Ireland reported that 80 per cent of third-level students had taken an illegal non-opiate drug (mainly cannabis) and over half were taking the drug at the time of the study (National Drugs Strategy, 2001, p. 33).

Other commentators have adopted a less sanguine view of young people's substance use. There is, they argue, some substance to the stereotype. Socio-demographic information on drug users as detailed in the National Drugs Strategy confirms the view that young men are more likely to experiment than are young women, a view confirmed by the UNODCCP, although this is beginning to change. Global data indicates that prevalence of drug use among the unemployed is significantly higher than for those in employment. In Britain, unemployed people were 32 per cent, and in the United States 40 per cent, more likely to use drugs than the employed were. Data from the Russian Federation indicated that 73 per cent of registered drug users were unemployed. Over three-quarters of drug users reporting for treatment in this country left school by the age of 16 years and over 70 per cent were unemployed (National Drugs Strategy 2001–2008, p. 22).

Harrison and Pottieger (1996), Dembo and Rivers (1996) and Browne et al. (1998) claim that there is growing evidence that sexual victimisation is strongly linked with substance abuse. They argue a strong cause-and-effect linkage between child sex abuse, serious familial malfunction and opiate use. They argue that young users often have serious multiple personal and family problems. Among the problems most consistently reported are physical abuse, sexual victimisation, poor emotional/ psychological and educational functioning and mental health problems. One of the women prisoners in Mountjoy in an interview stated that sexual abuse was the source of her drug use:

> I started to use drugs when I was nine. I was sexually abused when I was a kid and, like I always struggled with that so I just used drugs to escape, you know, started abusing solvents in school and that . . . (Dillon, 2001, p. 36)

Dembo and Rivers (1996) argue that the social environment in which drug users live is often "stressed" and that the psychological strain experienced by young people increases their risk of substance use, a view that is shared by Wacquant (1993), Morgan (2001) and Bourgois (1995). Bourgois claims that "substance abuse in the inner city is merely a symptom of deeper dynamics of social marginalisation and alienation" (p. 2). Stressful life events have also been identified by Plant and Plant (1992) as an important factor in initiating young people into drug use. However, they go on to say that it is often extremely difficult to tell whether stress is a cause or a result of alcohol or drug use. The stress or strain theory is itself inadequate as an explanation as to why some people in disadvantaged communities are attracted to drugs and some are not. Social disorganisation, deprivation, poverty, crime, unemployment and early school leaving are all predictors of stressful lives and the sequential strain can trigger serious and debilitating drug use within certain individuals.

These stresses and vulnerabilities, allied to the feelings of rejection and isolation, often result in enraged, violent young people, cut adrift from any stabilising forces. Such is the scenario in East Harlem as described by Bourgois (1995). In this world of inner-city desolation, "the vulnerable prey on one another"

(p. 272) lashing out violently and indiscriminately against whomsoever. In the process, drug addicts become agents not only in their own destruction but also in the destruction of their families and their communities. Their alienation feeds others people's alienation. The criminal actions in which drug-cracked youths are forced to engage to feed the habit pose a greater threat to others than the actual drugs themselves. The vulnerable in East Harlem are not alone in this respect.

In addition to these stressful situations, some commentators (Morgan, 2001) argue that some people are more prone to addiction than others as a result of the addictions of their parents. Sher (1991) argues that "children of alcoholics inherit temperamental personalities and increased pharmacological sensitivity" (cited in Morgan, 2001, p. 22). This sensitivity, allied to the social and emotional stress and strains that are the daily destiny of many young people living in deprived communities, increase the likelihood of experimentation becoming more than just a passing fad.

The clear division, as outlined in Chapter Two, between US and EU (with the exception of UK) policy is reflected in how drug users are perceived. For the most part, Europeans take a more benign view of the drug user. Inciardi (2000, pp. 197–8) seems to typify the more belligerent, individualised American perspective with the following description of the "typical" user:

> Inadequate, with pervasive feelings of inability to cope with needs, feelings of helplessness, inability to plan ahead, frequent feelings of despair, negativism, cynicism, diffuse anxiety, the perception of tasks as likely to lead to failure rather than success and a disproportionate fear of failure, immaturity, inability to postpone gratification, irresponsibility preoccupation with concrete and immediate objects, limited social skills, lack of ability to articulate feelings, failure to conform to norms of personal hygiene, vocationally maladjusted, overly suggestible, tough, smart, troublesome, excitable, hedonistic, antisocial, manipulative, selfish and petulant.

While there is little doubt, according to Parker (1999), that some such people exist, the damage is as much caused by underlying structural factors of poor education, housing and life opportunities and denial of human rights as it is by psychoactive excesses. It would, he argues, be much more appropriate to develop strategies and programmes for such young people within a framework of social exclusion, poverty and inequality than to pander to what he calls "tabloid opinion with sound bites" (1999, p. 162).

It is clear that users cannot be dichotomised between harmless recreational users on the one hand and hardened addicts on the other. Rather, use of drugs is best represented on a continuum with very infrequent, low risk at one end of the continuum and life-threatening, familially destructive, community-shattering abuse at the other. In between there is even the suggestion that some drug use is actually good for one's level of well-being. The life circumstances and consequences of serious and debilitating drug use have been well documented and will come as no real surprise. However, that that is not the full story will surprise many and certainly challenges the drug-using equals bad, no-drug-using equals good dichotomy and will surprise many.

Inevitably, how one names the user will largely determine how one responds to their needs. Some commentators, while agreeing with the continuum analogy, still insist in pointing out that even the infrequent, low-risk users are acting outside the law and contributing to the illicit wealth creation of unscrupulous drug barons. Others insist that low-risk use frequently leads to addictive use. The National Drugs Strategy 2001–2008 states that "the progression of use from tobacco and alcohol to cannabis and, then, to other drugs is a consistent finding in a number of studies on young people" (2001, p. 31).

Clearly, not everyone accepts the progression paradigm and it would appear that the empirical evidence in support of this view is scant. Not everyone who takes a drink becomes an alcoholic. Not everyone who uses cannabis becomes a heroin addict and not everyone who experiments with drugs becomes a drug addict. If that were the case, the estimated 185 million people in the world who consume illicit drugs would be in serious difficulty or, closer to home, the 2.4 per cent of the population of this country who use ecstasy would be in serious difficulty.

AGE PROFILE OF DRUG USERS

It is clear that people of all ages use drugs. It is equally clear that the focus of both politicians and policy-makers is on the habits of young people and within that cohort, as outlined above, on disadvantaged young people in communities that have been sorely neglected by policy makers. Less concern is focused on the use of licit drugs such as tranquillisers or pain-killers — the acceptable addiction of what Barker (1998, p. 61) calls "the silent but moral majority".

Plant et al. (1985, p. 2) emphasise the importance of acknowledging that "misuse is not, nor ever has been the sole prerogative of young people". The average age in Britain of those admitted as inpatients to psychiatric hospitals for alcohol dependence is over 40. Most of those receiving prescriptions for valium, librium and avian are middle-aged and elderly. Fatal drug doses are most common, not among the young, but among the elderly. The elderly are big consumers of prescribed drugs. Chetley (1995) estimates that the elderly consume at least 30 per cent of all prescribed drugs, many of them consuming a number of different drugs each day. Chetley argues that

> all the consequences of polypharmacy — increased costs, adverse drug reactions (ADR), and drug abuse and misuse are more likely to occur in the elderly than in any other group. (1995, p. 29)

Much of the over-prescribing is the result of the pathologising of age and the natural process of ageing and dying.

Tranquillisers and sleeping pills are consumed in huge numbers. In the United States, 1.5 million elderly people have been on minor tranquillisers daily for one year or more, and more than 500,000 elderly people use sleeping pills daily for one month or more (Chetley, 1995, p. 33). Older people's capacity to build toxins in the body is greater than the rest of the population due to reduced kidney activity, therefore increasing the risks attached to high drug consumption.

Such rampant consumption results in serious consequences for the aged, in many cases decreasing rather than increasing their level of well-being. Chetley (1995) estimates that anything between 10 and 20 per cent of elderly admissions to hospitals are due to over-prescribing and over-consumption. He claims that doctors are over-reliant on promotional material sent by the drug companies. Many of the drugs prescribed for older people were never tested for use by older people and therefore cannot cope with the different rate of metabolism, increased body fat or reduced blood flow that are common among the elderly.

In spite of what Plant et al. (1985, p. 2) call "this catalogue of woes", disproportionate attention, they argue, has been given to drug use of young people. However, in terms of illicit drug use, there is clear evidence worldwide that prevalence is higher among the younger age group than among the older age group. Evidence from the United States indicates that illicit drug consumption peaks at 18–20 years of age.

Within the youth cohort who use drugs, there is the view that young people who experiment with drugs early in life, certainly those who experiment under the age of sixteen, are more likely to go on and abuse other drugs and this likelihood increases as poverty and social alienation increases. According to Brook and Brook (1996, p. 37), "the major period of risk for initiation into the use of illegal drugs is over by the age of twenty". Early experimentation with alcohol and cigarettes are indicators of later drug use. However, according to Shiner and Newburn (1999, p. 143), repeated surveys in Britain show that experimentation is rare during early teen years but that it increases sharply in mid-teens, peaking in late teens and early twenties.

Harrison and Pottieger (1996, p. 130) regard alcohol and cigarettes as "gateway drugs" or, as Barker (1998, p. 61) describes them, "demon drugs" enticing users into "deeper and deeper depths of addiction, despair and depravity" or later soft to hard drug use. This view resonates strongly with some and is strongly contested by others. Alcohol, they argue, provides an early experience with being high and cigarette use entails what they refer to as "most of the skills needed" to get high from smoking other substances. Other studies referred to in the National Drugs Strategy 2001–2008 (p. 39) reinforce this view.

In focusing on the young and the marginalised, both policy makers and politicians can create an environment where the users are the "other", separate from the rest of society and by implication "normal" society. Users who are individualised out from family, community and broader society are easy prey to portrayals of being a threat to society and in the process justifying a "zero tolerance" towards their behaviour. Thus the dehumanising process begins. The young become scumbags, scroungers and wasters, easy prey to those who wish to criminalise all illicit drug users.

Youth drug use is further problematised/criminalised in a way that older people's drug use is not, primarily because of its association with anti-social behaviour. Concern about youth drug use has, according to the National Drugs Strategy 2001–2008, "long been a major concern, not least because of the threat to public health, but also because of the strong relationship between alcohol and drug misuse and anti-social and criminal behaviour" (2001, p. 28). The implication could be taken that the real problem is not so much the drug use but the risks to public health and the anti-social behaviour. The lower level of attention given to third-level drug-using students adds substance to the view that drug-taking amongst young people in third-level colleges will be tolerated in a way that drug-taking by other young people is not.

GENDERING OF DRUG USE

As in all other areas of society, both consumption patterns and society's understanding and reaction to drug use is highly gendered. Underpinning the bulk of the literature is a belief that drug use is essentially a male "problem". Research and anecdotal evidence would tend to give credence to this view. Boys and men are more likely to consume drugs in public places and control the distribution networks. Prosecutions in the courts tend to support the view that men are more likely than are women to be at the top of the drug hierarchy, in the same way as men are at the top of the political and economic hierarchies.

While male drug users continue to outnumber female users, Geoghegan et al. (1999) claim that "the number of female drug users is increasing at a faster rate in many countries than it is for males" (Geoghegan et al., 1999, p. 134), a view shared by

Morgan (2001). The UNODCCP Report also supports this assertion. According to the report, "worldwide drug abuse continues
to be more widespread among males than females, even
though several countries reported increases in female abuse
levels over the past couple of years" (UNODCCP, 2002, p. 213).
The UNODCCP report that 84 per cent of all registered drug
users in the Russian Federation are male, 80 per cent in the CIS
countries (former Soviet Union), 83 per cent in Bolivia and 80
per cent in Colombia. In more developed countries, there is
clear evidence of an increase in the number of women users.
The figure for females in the UK and Germany is 37 per cent
and in the US 44 per cent. International statistics also indicate
significant gender differences in the type of drug consumed.
Women are more likely to consume tranquillisers, sedatives,
analgesics and stimulant-anorectics while men are more likely
to consume heroin, crack cocaine and methamphetamine (a derivative of amphetamine but with quicker and longer action;
amphetamine is a synthetic stimulant and decongestant drug).

Henderson (1999) reviewing early feminist writings on
drugs states that the dominant construction of female drug use
was that of victim where drugs were perceived as yet another
weapon of subjection in the arsenal of patriarchy. Everyday life
is characterised as a struggle, with men having greater access
to economic, social, cultural and sexual power and consequently being the agents of women's oppression. All of these
factors are to be found in prostitution. Here men's privilege and
sexual power coalesce to the detriment of women. The oppression of women was not confined to the illegal dealers. Many
feminists argued that the over-prescribing of drugs, particularly valium, by doctors was on a par with street dealers. The
intention of both, they argued, was to pacify and control.

Irish research tended to support the gendered analysis. The
Mid-Western Health Board report on prostitution identifies alcohol and drug use as factors that contribute to both women
and men becoming prostitutes (1998, p. 2). As well as being
contributory factors in drawing people into prostitution, alcohol
and drug use are also the result of prostitution, as many of the
sex trade workers try to cope with the harsh reality of their
lives. The National Drugs Strategy Report 2001–2008 (2001,

p. 36) reports on a *Women's Health Project of the Eastern Health Board Report* (1999) that highlighted the high level of polydrug use amongst prostitutes. The report also highlighted the link between drug use and poverty, reporting that 83 per cent were working in prostitution because of financial need. This finding is in keeping with international findings that indicate high consumption patterns among sex workers. In Vietnam and Cambodia, for example, prevalence of drug use and corresponding high levels of HIV/AIDS were found among sex workers in a study conducted in 1998 (UNAIDS/WHO, 2002), findings that can be replicated in many other developing countries.

Other research challenges this view. The emergence of the phenomenon of "girl power", whether a media creation or of real significance, challenges some of the more traditional perspectives in the belief "that sisters were now doing it for themselves". Henderson (1999) from her research on 3,000 young women aged 13–19 concluded that:

> Women were evidently not being frog-marched into drug use by men and were not leading deeply unhappy lives as a result of their drug use. The young post-modern woman knows what she wants on and off the dance floor. (Henderson, 1999, pp. 41–2)

Their drug use was, she argues, "only one part of buying into a lifestyle to which pleasure was central".

Insofar as it can be assumed that pleasure and the pursuit of pleasure is the driving force of this generation of female experimenters, it can be assumed that pleasure-seeking is also the driving force of male experimentation. However, Henderson (1999) cautions policy-makers about assuming that women's use of drugs and official responses to women's consumption patterns are on a par with men's. Women, she argues, take it easier with drugs and she claims they seem to get a better "buzz". She goes on to say that the solutions which policy-makers apply to boys and men do not have the same resonance for girls and women.

Challenging Henderson's (1999) assertion that "sisters are doing it for themselves", Geoghegan et al. (1999) claim that women users experience greater difficulty finding injecting sites and are more likely to need someone else to help with injecting. They also argue that in terms of consequences of severe drug use, the rate of physical and mental deterioration is more rapid among injecting women. Women are, they argue, "more likely to report suffering from mental health problems such as depression, anxiety and feeling unable to cope and feeling isolated" (2000, p. 134). The Annual Report on the State of the Drug Problem in the European Union indicates that mortality rates among female opiate users are higher then their male counterparts. The Report claims that overdoses, accidents, suicide and infectious diseases contribute to the overall high level (EMCDDA, 2001, p. 19).

While agreeing with Henderson (1999) that women's drug use is highly gendered and that responses should reflect that, in all other respects Geoghegan et al. (1999), Bourgois (1995) and Murphy-Lawless (2002) strongly contest Henderson's upbeat assessment of women's experiences of drugs. Their view is closer to that of early feminist writers on drugs, as outlined above. Based on a study of 934 new attendees at a Dublin syringe exchange clinic, Geoghegan et al. (1999) claim that women are more at risk from infection with human immunodeficiency virus (HIV) and hepatitis because women are more likely to have a sexual partner who is an injecting user and more likely to share equipment and drug paraphernalia. Furthermore, they claim that women are more likely to engage in risk behaviour than their male counterparts.

Bourgois's (1995) ethnographic study of Puerto Ricans living in East Harlem depicts a street culture of misogyny, use, abuse, neglect, regular violence, disempowerment, dislocation and exclusion. Women's place within drug-saturated communities like East Harlem is defined by patriarchal parameters. They are often subjected to harrowing violence. They are regularly denigrated by the men in their lives — generally referred to as "bitches". Yet these same men very often depend on them for food and shelter for themselves, while expecting that they will fulfil their traditional maternal role and take responsibility for the children — a dependency that Murphy-Lawless (2002) also found in inner-city Dublin.

Women's exclusion from street enterprises is governed by the same kind of patriarchal values that dictate mainstream

employment. While street dealing and its related activities provides an alternative economy for people who find it very difficult, if not impossible, to gain acceptance in the mainstream
capitalist environment, that outlet remains very much the prerogative of men. Women are excluded from "the more profit-
able, autonomous entrepreneurial niches such as dealing,
mugging and burglarising" by the male-dominated ranks of the
underground (Bourgois, 1995, p. 280). Prostitution remains one
of the few sources of income-generating activities for drug-
using women. Consequently, the 1980s crack explosion in New
York and other cities was matched by a huge increase in the
number of drug-addicted women in prostitution, causing an
epidemic of venereal diseases among young women and new-
born babies in the inner city.

Given the level of control that women in these circumstances exert over their own bodies, it is not surprising that the
level of pregnancy among young drug-addicted prostitutes is
high. The EMCDDA estimate that the rate of pregnancy among
young women drug users is higher than in the general population. They believe this may be explained by factors such as
"promiscuity, prostitution and irregular use of contraception"
(EMCDDA, 2001, p. 3). Results from a Red Cross project in Bar-
celona (ibid.) indicate that the pregnant drug users are more
likely to have premature births, miscarriages and, not unex-
pectedly, higher levels of HIV.

The misogyny witnessed by Bourgois is not just a recent
phenomenon, nor is it confined to the streets of East Harlem.
Walton (2001) claims that not only is drug use highly gendered
but so too are society's responses. He claims that the Habitual
Inebriates Act of 1898 was used disproportionately against
women, "those fallen women who had incurred the wrath of the
law through prostitution . . . neglectful mothers, neglectful of
their children or indeed of their duty to bear children for the
propagation of the Empire" (Walton, 2001, p. 199).

Bourgois (1995) reports on editorials in the *New York Times*
that slammed women for their neglect of their maternal instincts
and for turning themselves into monsters. The reality is so very
different. Murphy-Lawless (2002) found very little evidence of
the mother-monster figure in her ethnographic study of "how

ordinary everyday life, specifically ordinary life for women, has been influenced by the growth of the illegal heroin culture and economy in the north inner city [of Dublin]" (Murphy-Lawless, 2002, p. 15).

Murphy-Lawless (2002) highlights the complexity of roles that women, and in particular mothers living in disadvantaged communities with high levels of drug use, have to juggle. In the north inner-city, women have encountered drugs as mothers, partners, sisters, daughters, as users themselves and as activists against the blight that drugs and the associated criminal activity has caused to the neighbourhoods where they live.

The overlapping nature of the multiplicity of roles that many women encounter adds enormous stress to already stressed lives. Murphy-Lawless (2002) claims that women experience a greater sense of failure and inadequacy when their children become addicted to heroin and this sense of failure is accentuated in the case of their daughters. Murphy-Lawless (2002) observed the level of pain, anguish and daily strain that such women experience:

> The central message that came through . . . was the extent to which women had worked hard to rear their children in extremely daunting circumstances . . . but as patterns of addiction emerged amongst sons and daughters, their mothers endured almost inexpressible anguish (2002, pp. 59–60).

What Henderson (1999), Geoghegan et al. (1999), Murphy-Lawless (2002) and Bourgois (1995) have in common is shared awareness and acknowledgement of women as drug users with particular if not homogenous needs. Equally, all are agreed that not only is men's experience of drugs significantly different but that they, like their counterparts in mainstream society, experience a patriarchal dividend.

Men's experiences of and reactions to drug use is significantly different to that of women, as has been alluded to above. Murphy-Lawless (2002) claims fathers of heroin users are less able/inclined to respond to their children's heroin addiction and take refuge in the pub. Bourgois (1995) paints a much bleaker picture of how masculinity is constructed in communities in thrall to drugs. Careful not to overly individualise

responsibility or to contribute to the cultural stereotyping of the
Puerto Rican community, he does not seek to pathologise individual actions. Rather, he seeks to accurately describe street
life as he experienced it, while keeping true to his structuralist
anti-racist analysis, without sanitising those he describes. He
relays stories of young men who routinely celebrate violence
and gratuitous cruelty, including gang rape. Reflecting on the
stories that he heard, Bourgois (1995) found it difficult to confront the extent of "gendered brutality" (1995, p. 207).

Street culture also takes for granted, Bourgois (1995) claims,
the right of fathers to abandon their children while they search
for drugs and status in the underground world. For a father to
abandon his children does not carry any social sanction; for a
mother to do likewise carries enormous sanction — "men decry
single mothers' failings as head of households, yet ignore their
own obligations for family sustenance" (Bourgois, 1995, p. 276).
Almost all of the men Bourgois encountered in East Harlem
were fathers but *none* contributed to the maintenance of their
children, while retaining a yearning, at least momentarily, for
their loss. Rather they "terrorised" (p. 287) their children and
the mothers of their children. For these men, masculine dignity
was not to be found in building relationships with their women
partners and children but in "promiscuity, conspicuous violence and ecstatic substance abuse" (Bourgois, 1995, p. 288).

For children growing up in communities where drug use is
prevalent, their life chances are considerably diminished.
Bourgois (1995) claims that the upsurge in crack consumption
was matched by a massive increase in child abuse and child
neglect. Children were taken into foster care in record-
breaking numbers in the mid-1980s. If the homes of children
were unsafe in the immediate aftermath of the introduction of
crack onto the streets of cities, the streets where children play
were not much safer. Murphy-Lawless (2002) reproaches Dublin Corporation for having failed over many years to renew play
areas and equipment in their flat complexes. What were formerly playgrounds became wastelands where toddlers and
young children were constantly at risk from cars, needles and
abandoned furniture. Bourgois (1995) concludes his ethnogra-
phy of life in East Harlem with the following poignant tableau:

> I still cannot forget the expression in the terrified, hapless
> eyes of the five-year-old boy who was watching his mother
> argue with a cocaine dealer at 2:00 a.m. in the stairway of a
> tenement where Primo and I had taken shelter from a thun-
> der shower on my second night back in the neighbourhood.
> Primo shrugged when I tried to discuss the plight of the
> child with him, "Yeah, Felipe, I know, I hate seeing that shit
> too. It's wack." (Bourgois, 1995, p. 337)

Any attempts the men in the *barrio* of East Harlem made to find
dignity or the all-important "respect" through the world of
mainstream work were thwarted. The cultural capital that
means survival on the street has very little currency in what
passes as the legal economy. With the demise of traditional
manual and the rise of office-based work, the information-
technology-dominated workplace requires a different sort of
cultural capital. In this setting, the linguistic skills, cultural values and street ways of interacting are given scant recognition.
Soon most become discouraged by the experience and leave to
return to the more familiar drug-dealing and other enterprises
of the street, where they create and mirror the exploitation in-
herent in mainstream capitalism. Drug-dealing and allied street
enterprises are statements both of defiance and resistance
against a society that has all but dismissed them. The tragedy is
that the defiance and resistance often result in such personal
and social destructiveness.

SOCIAL CLASS AND DRUGS

Control and prohibition of alcohol and drug use is, according to
Walton (2001), intrinsically linked to social class. Juxtaposing
Ancient Greece with the football terraces of England in the
1980s, Walton claims that the objective in restricting some people's access to drugs and alcohol through licensing or outright
prohibition is to increase surveillance and control and impose
behaviour modification on those who may pose a threat to the
establishment.

Social class is a key variable in relation to both consumption
and response to patterns of use. The evidence suggests that the
state subjects working-class communities to greater levels of

surveillance and lower levels of tolerance when it comes to drug use. The evidence also suggests that social class also needs to be a key variable in any response that is being planned to address the fall-out from serious and debilitating drug use in working-class communities.

While community development is key to addressing drug use and social and economic disadvantage, how community development is constructed and mediated is crucial. The involvement and role of such workers as agents of change in working-class communities is strongly contested. The tension is not just as a result of interpersonal differences or of squabbles over who gets paid and who does not — important and all as that debate is — but extends to the power relations between local activists and professional facilitators and state or voluntary agencies.

When working-class communities are resourced, there is the view that outside agencies and individuals are the main beneficiaries. Many communities require professional full-time support workers in their various struggles and sometimes there is a value in the support worker with fresh eyes and ears coming from outside the community. Understandably, however, there is often resistance to what are perceived as parachuted workers who have no prior relationship with the area being funded while local people who have been grafting for long periods beforehand are not deemed worthy of payment. Given the current and growing emphasis on professionalisation and accreditation, local communities are very sensitive about who gets paid for engaging in drug and community work and who does not. Many people in deprived communities never had the opportunity to access education and training and therefore do not have the qualifications that state and other service providers are demanding. Even when working-class people have broken through the glass ceiling that inhibits their educational mobility, the very education they receive can undermine their class identity or else those with whom they grew up may now perceive them differently.

Dorgan and McDonnell (1997) not only challenge the role and impact of such facilitators and outside agencies but also the broader issue of the relationship between working-class people and those who use the lives of the working class as "gristto-the-mill of academic middle class professional discourse" (Dorgan and McDonnell, 1997, p. 72). Such workers often "take up positions of power in defining others" (p. 73) resulting in the further disempowerment and marginalisation of working-class people. McVeigh (2002) also challenges the involvement of middle-class professionals' role in working-class communities. He argues that "communities develop through struggle — not through the good offices of professional middle class community workers who parachute in to develop them like garden vegetables" (McVeigh, 2002, p. 53).

ETHNICITY AND DRUG USE

Within the EU and Europe generally, drug use is believed to be fairly prevalent among some socially and economically marginalised ethnic groups who are even more cut-off from service provision due to language and cultural reasons. For obvious reasons, the precise level of drug use is difficult to establish. Minority ethnic groups' caution around mainstream authority figures, the fear of being scapegoated, nomadism, language barriers, all combine to make drug use estimates more difficult. A study conducted by the University of Middlesex in England from September 1999 to November 2000 revealed that countries "rarely make specific provision for minorities within their national drug strategy" (EMCDDA, March–April, 2001, p. 2).

Reflecting on the interplay between ethnicity, race and exclusion, Khan (2000) challenges popular stereotypical images of ethnic minorities as habitual drug users. While acknowledging that very little is known at EU level about social exclusion, drugs and minorities, what data there is does not support such a view, she contends. Despite this, Khan claims that "minorities are over-represented amongst drug-law offenders reported to the judicial system" (Khan, 2000, p. 9). Khan also asserts that national, regional and local drug policies are generally silent on the issue of drugs and minorities. While addressing the situation of Travellers and the homeless as at-risk groups, the National Drugs Strategy 2001–2008 makes no reference to the situation of newly arrived residents from different ethnic backgrounds, some of whom are living in inner-city areas, places worst affected by heroin use.

Given the marginalised and branded spaces that members of the Travelling community inhabit and the level of exclusion and discrimination they experience, it would be expected from studies of other marginalised groups in other countries that levels of substance abuse would be high. A study conducted for Pavee Point (Hurley, 1999) highlights some significant differences between drug use within the Traveller community and the settled community. The research indicated that "while the age of commencement was higher than the settled population at around 16/17, substance use persisted into early adulthood" (Hurley, 1999, p. 16).

In keeping with trends in the settled community, there were clear gender differences in drug use within the Traveller community. Young Traveller men who are particularly at risk include those who are housed with settled people in disadvantaged areas, children of parents who have substance abuse problems and those who have a history of offending and have spent time in prisons.

Traveller women were, according to the study, often introduced into drug use by their husbands/partners and as a consequence their introduction was at a later age, notwithstanding the young age at which many members of the Traveller community marry. While cannabis remains the main illegal drug of use within the Traveller community, many women Travellers were using significant amounts of prescribed drugs. According to the Report, the use of prescription tranquillisers and sedatives for women Travellers has become normalised "as many doctors, who perhaps felt that they could not respond to the pressures faced by young Traveller women living in difficult social circumstances, the easy answer was to prescribe drugs as an immediate response" (Hurley, 1999, p. 17).

Heroin use amongst the Travelling community is apparently confined in the main to men. As in the settled community, it is the very disadvantaged Travellers who are most at risk from heroin use. But all Traveller drug use is linked to their overall status in society. Despite recent legislation, most notably the Equal Status Act 2000, many members of the Travelling community find it difficult to get served in bars and hotels. As a consequence, cannabis has become normalised as a psychoactive substance within the community. Equally, many members of the Travelling community are excluded from the mainstream paid workforce through discriminatory practices and so, like the Puerto Ricans in East Harlem as described above, recourse to the illegal trade in drugs offers to some the only perceived way of earning a living in the alternative economy.

In addressing the issue of ethnicity and drugs, there are obvious dangers. Given the recent arrival of relatively large numbers of people from a diverse range of ethnic backgrounds, the risk of scapegoating people from ethnic minorities and feeding into racist and xenophobic feelings cannot be underestimated. Yet ethnicity issues do, as outlined above, influence drug use. Given the level of ghettoisation and enforced idleness as a result of the present government's asylum work and housing policies, the temptation to turn to drugs as a coping mechanism cannot be disregarded. This potential market cannot have escaped the attention of entrepreneurial drug dealers. Policies and practices need to reflect that.

RACE, RACISM AND DRUGS

Bourgois claims that "mainstream society easily evokes racial stereotypes to dismiss drug addicts as pathetic losers or as lazy, pathological self-destructive drug addicts" (1995, p. 137). Racism is about the construction of Black, Asian and Hispanic people as different from White people as the other, the stranger, as someone who either individually or collectively will threaten, dilute or "chocolatise" (browning the population) the White population. Agreeing with the concept of otherness, Coomber argues that the notion of the other as threat or danger not only feeds xenophobic racist leanings but reflects them as well (Coomber, 1998, p. *xii*).

Racism is constructed from opposites, "them" and "us". While Western Caucasian people are no more likely to be racist than are other groups of people, their racism has more of an impact as Caucasians control more of the resources of the world than do other groups. Caucasian racism is often grounded in a fear of counter-colonisation, domination and dilution of the world that White people have constructed. The production and distribution of illegal drugs is often presented as one of the ways in which Black, Asian and Hispanic peoples undermine the Caucasian world.

Michael Woodiwiss argues that initial moves to prohibit the use of drugs were rooted in racism and fear of interracial contact, thereby threatening the "purity, even the survival of the white race" (1998, p. 14). The Chinese were the first targets. In 1881, San Francisco police reported finding "white women and Chinese men side by side under the effects of drugs — a humiliating sight to anyone with anything left of manhood" (1998, p. 14). In 1910, the Report on the International Opium Commission claimed that cocaine made rapists of Black men and that Blacks achieved immense strength and cunning under its influence. Blacks and Chinese were considered the drug carriers while the Caucasians were their young targets. Henry J. Anslinger, the commissioner of the Federal Bureau of Narcotics, included in one of his reports descriptions of "coloured students partying with white female students, smoking and getting sympathy with stories of racial persecution resulting in pregnancy" (Woodiwiss, 1998, p. 23).

In Britain, the death of actress Billie Carlton in 1918 was seen as one of the catalysts marking the introduction of legal restrictions on the sale and consumption of drugs. Concern at her death was, according to Kohn (Mott and Bean, 1998), partly racially motivated. Intense press coverage followed her death, setting a trend that was to be the hallmark for the rest of the century. Tales of opium, heroin and cocaine use among the artistic circle filled the newspapers in what is regarded as the pre-tabloid era. Of particular concern was the "corruption of young women [as a result of] mixing together currents of dope, sexual perversion, fornication and miscegenation" (Mott and Bean, 1998, p. 35). White women were, according to Walton, perceived to be "vulnerable to their black and yellow skinned companions and the carnal rapacity of the obscenely endowed Negro and the vile hyper-imaginative sadism of the Chinaman" (2001, p. 165). Such pornographic images are not confined to the past. Bourgois (1995) claims that "the fantasy of [Black and

Hispanic] crack-gorged women being propelled by insatiable sexual cravings is shared by journalists, social scientists, dealers and addicts themselves" (1995, p. 280).

Equally, the often alleged but wholly unsubstantiated allegation of the deliberate infecting of Black and, in the context of the United States, African American peoples with AIDS and other illnesses is perceived as the Caucasian attempt to undermine their counter-colonisation surge. Medicine and the use and abuse of legal drugs are perceived to be part of the arsenal of White people in their racial war against Black people. Historically, there is some basis for these fears. Dr J. Marion Sims, who is regarded as the father of gynaecology in the United States, "used black women slaves to perfect his procedures to repair vaginal fistulas" (Reverby, 2001, p. 23). Reverby (2001) goes on to detail accounts of the remains of Black people being robbed from graves in what has been labelled as a "form of post-mortem racism in nineteenth century training" (Reverby, 2001, p. 23).

The hugely controversial Tuskegee Study — *Untreated Syphilis in the Male Negro* — of 399 African American men who had contracted syphilis dating from 1932 until 1972 is the twentieth-century equivalent of what took place a century earlier. The circumstances in which the men contracted the disease, and what happened to them subsequently, have entered the realm of folklore and have come to serve various narratives about the way western medicine colonises Black bodies for research purposes. Reverby (2001) claims that the evidence only partially supports the allegation that the men were deliberately infected with syphilis and then left untreated so that the progression of the disease could be monitored. Whatever about the circumstances in which the disease was contracted, that the men were left untreated while being given the opposite impression is now unchallenged. The men were given placebos, aspirin or just vitamin pills in lieu of penicillin. The men were simply never told that they were part of an experiment that would try and deny them treatment for their disease.

> The Public Health Service did many things to keep the men from treatment: tracking them to other public health departments across the country, intervening with local physi-

cians and even the local draft board, perpetuating the falsi-
fication that they were being treated by providing aspirins
and vitamins and lying. (Reverby, 2001, p. 24)

Eventually the truth emerged and the participants in the study
received a fulsome presidential apology in 1997.

> So today America does remember the hundreds of men
> used in research without their knowledge and consent. Men
> who were poor and African American, without resources
> and with few alternatives. They were betrayed. They were
> lied to by their government. The United States government
> did something that was wrong — deeply, profoundly, mor-
> ally wrong. It was an outrage. What the United States gov-
> ernment did was shameful, and I am sorry. You were
> grievously wronged. I apologise and I am sorry that this
> apology has been so long in coming. To our African Ameri-
> can citizens, I am sorry that your federal government or-
> chestrated a study so clearly racist. (Clinton, 1997)

Whether that marks the end of drug testing and medical experimentation on African American and other racial minorities
remains a moot point. Certainly allegations of further abuses
are commonplace. Philippe Bourgois (1995), in his ethnographic study of crack use in East Harlem, New York, provides
an account of Black and Hispanic children in residential educational centres for disturbed children which would suggest otherwise, as the following extract indicates:

> They had us in school on Ward's Island for Special Educa-
> tion. Ward's island is where they keep all the lunatics. They
> had everybody on Thorazine there. They used to experi-
> ment with Thorazine on the Spanish and black kids. That was
> the testing ground for those drugs. They had kids on all
> kinds of drugs. Word up. (Bourgois, 1995, p. 190)

Bourgois's study spells out in graphic detail the social, community, familial and individual reality of addiction while recognising that substance use in the inner city is merely a symptom of
social marginalisation and alienation. He was a witness to "the
maelstrom consuming children (and their friends and families)
on the street" (Bourgois, 1995, p. 272). The concomitant illegal

enterprises that inner city residents are forced into "embroils most of its participants in lifestyles of violence, substance abuse and internalised rage . . . ultimately leading to personal degradation and community ruin" (Bourgois, 1995, p. 9).

The experience of the Puerto Rican residents in East Harlem is to be found again and again in inner-city areas right across the globe as evidenced in, for example, Wacquant's (1993) comparative study of the black American ghetto and the French urban ghetto. Wacquant (1993) claims that European poverty and drug abuse is becoming Americanised, that many European inner-city residents are caught in similar maelstroms.

Like their American counterparts, those on the margins in Europe, along with the newly arrived and first, second and third generations of peoples from former colonised countries in Africa, Eastern Europe and Asia are confined to stigmatised areas. Many of these areas are "publicly recognised as dumping grounds for poor people, downwardly mobile working class households and marginalised groups and individuals" (Wacquant, 1993, p. 368). With little hope and without the social, economic or cultural capital — which finds ready acceptance in western culture — to radically alter their life chances, drugs both legal and illegal provide a temporary relief from what Wacquant calls "neighbourhoods of exile" (1993, p. 369).

Certainly, persistent and addictive drug use is costly both in terms of real and opportunity costs and the absence of these opportunities forces some people to turn to crime. In turn these people and these areas are viewed with feeling of insecurity in the mainly white affluent suburbs. Collectively and individually, people living in these areas are the perceived threat because of their poverty, ethnicity, un(der)employed status, allied in some cases to serious drug use. The fear is as much fear of "the other" as much as it is of the drugs per se. Bourgois argues that "mainstream society easily evokes racial stereotypes to dismiss drug addicts as pathetic losers or as lazy pathological self-destructive drug addicts" (1995, p. 137). For Bourgois, race rather than drug consumption is the starting point of rejection.

Compared to the United States, Ireland is only at the starting blocks when it comes to confronting the seemingly inevitable tensions associated with multicultural societies. Serious concern has been expressed at the level of racism directed at newly arrived residents from outside the EU. This concern has been expressed by asylum-seekers, refugees and other newly arrived non-nationals, by the small indigenous Black population and by many agencies, most notably Amnesty International.

Two developments of note have taken place in this country in the last five years: firstly, the increase in the numbers of newly arrived people into this state, and secondly, recent equality legislation protecting the rights of minorities. In 1998 and 1999, there were 12,373 applications for refugee status in this country, of which 224 were recognised as refugees at first instance and a further 666 were recognised on appeal. In addition there were 2,214 programme refugees and 209 people were granted leave to remain on humanitarian grounds. A further 1,227 applicants were granted permission to remain in the State on parentage grounds and 2,239 people were granted post-nuptial citizenship in the same two years (these grounds for remaining in the country were overturned by the Supreme Court in 2003). Romanians and Nigerians topped the asylum application tables in 1998 and 1999 with Poland, the Democratic Republic of the Congo, Moldova, Libya and Algeria next in line. In the same two years, 7,915 work visas were issued. Indonesia, Jordan and Malaysia topped the non-western countries whose citizens were granted visas in 1998 and Brazil, India and Latvia topped the table in 1999 (Ward, 2001, pp. 7–24). To what extent all of this and the recent legislation impacted on drug policy has yet to be established.

The record of international police forces in relation to their dealings with ethnic minorities, most particularly with Black and Hispanic peoples is not impressive. Davenport-Hines (2001, p. 363) claims that "75 per cent of arrests for cocaine and crack offences involved Black people whereas 80 per cent in Lewisham of cocaine and crack users known to drug agencies and social services were White". The Stephen Lawrence case in England and the Rodney King case in Los Angeles were just two high-profile cases that highlight police racial bias. At the inquiry into the Stephen Lawrence murder, Lord Scarman stated that:

the damage done by even the occasional display of racial prejudice is incalculable. It is therefore essential that every possible step be taken to prevent and to root out racially prejudiced attitudes in the police service. The police cannot rest on the argument that since they are a cross-section of society some officers are bound to be racially prejudiced. In this respect, as in others, the standards we apply to the police must be higher than the norms of behaviour prevalent in society as a whole. (MacPherson, 1999, Section 6.9)

Currently all the evidence in the US suggests that African and Hispanic Americans are disproportionately more likely to be arrested, convicted and sentenced for drug offences than are Caucasians. African Americans are now five times more likely to be arrested on drug charges than are Caucasian males. The Washington DC-based Sentencing Project found that "25 per cent of African American males in their twenties are either in prison, on parole or probation: the figure for Caucasians were six per cent and for Hispanics ten per cent" (Woodiwiss, 1998, p. 28).

In such a context of well-documented racism within police forces, particularly in the United States and Britain (Giddens, 1993, p. 278; McGregor, 1998, p. 152), comments by Garda Commissioner Patrick Byrne at the Patrick McGill Summer School (2001) give rise for concern. At the McGill School, Commissioner Byrne rhetorically asked, "What do we aspire to as a *normal* Irish society"? (Byrne, 2001, p. 8, *emphasis added*). He went on to ask, "should the drug-taking culture of the Far East, India and North Africa be imposed here?" (Byrne, 2001, p. 8).

The extent to which the Commissioner's comment will feed perceptions that the Gardaí are unsympathetic to people from minority ethnic groups remains a moot point. The Amnesty International report (2001) raises serious issues regarding policing and racism, despite the existence of the Garda Racism and Intercultural Unit. Listing areas in the world where many of these people come from, as a potential threat to our culture, does not contribute to the creation of intercultural understanding and harmony. Given the government's commitment to combat racism through informing public opinion and promoting a more tolerant inclusive society, there is an onus on senior public figures to ensure that, in so far as possible, their public statements do not in any way give succour to those within society who wish to perpetuate racial suspicions and divisions.

Given that as a society we are still only beginning to feel our way in this latest manifestation of a multicultural environment — historically Ireland has experienced many different influxes of people from the English, the Normans and the Vikings and those that preceded them — it is imperative that simplistic juxtapositions between race and drugs are avoided and that drug scaremongering is never racially tinged.

SEXUAL ORIENTATION AND DRUG USE

Sexual orientation is also regarded as a strong predictor of drug use and this applies in particular to gay men. An Anglo-American market research company reported that "gay men are almost five times more likely to abuse substances than their straight counterparts — gay men, perhaps more than any other group in British society, are polydrug users" (Tierney, 2002, p. 41).

Irish gay men are equally more likely to use drugs than are their straight counterparts and their consumption is on a par with their English gay counterparts. In a study of 1,269 gay men published in June 2002 (Carroll et al.), 55 per cent of those surveyed had consumed an illicit drug other than alcohol, Viagra or steroids. Apart from alcohol, over 38 per cent of gay men consumed Nitrites or "Poppers" (both Amyl Nitrite and Butyl Nitrite poppers get their name from the popping sound they made when first used in medicine — they came in a small glass capsule covered in cotton wool which was crushed between the fingers, resulting in a popping noise). As well as being used by the gay community, they are used by ravers and other club goers to accompany dance drugs such as amphetamines and ecstasy. Ecstasy is also a drug of choice amongst the gay community with just over 25 per cent of the gay men surveyed stating that they used it. Gay men are, however, more likely to use cannabis (32.5 per cent) than ecstasy. Cocaine and speed (amphetamines), drugs that speed up the way your body works — hence its name — are consumed by 14 per cent and over 12 per cent respectively.

No comparative study was found for lesbian women, although anecdotal evidence would suggest that there is a higher incidence of alcohol use/abuse among lesbians than there is among their heterosexual counterparts. There is a perceptible dearth of research and funding for research on this group of the population.

International research among the gay community indicates levels of high-risk behaviour. A survey of gay/bisexual men in Kazakhstan found that 9 per cent also injected intravenously and only 3 per cent used a condom, significantly increasing the risk to themselves and to those with whom they had sexual contact. A similar pattern has emerged in studies in Latin America. According to UNAIDS/WHO, "unsafe sex among men who have sex with men is rife across the region" (UNAIDS/WHO, 2002, p. 20). The report indicates high incidences (13 per cent) of HIV amongst gay/bisexual men in Honduras with low condom use and low perception of risk. The study found even higher levels in the South American cities of Lima (14 per cent), Bogotá (20 per cent) and Guayaquil (28 per cent).

A structural analysis of this level of consumption would suggest that it is linked to the level of homophobia that exists in society. If some working-class people are driven to inordinate levels of drug use because of high levels of alienation, resulting from the marginalised space they occupy in society, equally feelings of alienation and concomitant low levels of self-esteem drive consumption levels within the gay community. Within this paradigm, stigma, denial, and discrimination all combine to increase the likelihood of drug use.

Tierney (2002) offers other explanations for the alleged high levels of consumption. Given that full gay expression is denied in mainstream society, it very often can only find full expression in safe areas like dedicated clubs and bars. As a reaction to the many constraints gay people encounter in their day-to-day living, gay expression is often associated with excesses like drug and alcohol consumption.

> Unlike mainstream society, the focal point of gay social life tends to occur in the up-all-night atmosphere of pubs, bars and night-clubs, where beer is sunk by the pint or five and

chemicals ingested like they are going out of fashion. (Tierney, 2002, p. 41)

Gay people tend to go out more, according to Tierney, so they
are more likely to be in contact with drugs. Unlike most of their
straight counterparts with children whose nightlife is curtailed
as a result, older gay and lesbians continue to frequent night-
clubs, so the age profile of the gay drug user tends to be older
than the average drug user. Within safe settings, the normal restrictions that gay and lesbian people are subjected to in terms
of self-expression are lifted and "the feeling of being put upon
(is replaced) by hedonistic drug use and celebration of life"
(Tierney, 2002, p. 41). Tierney also claims that gay people have
warmed to drug use with enthusiasm. It would appear that in
this setting, the normalisation theory finds full expression.

INTRAVENOUS DRUG USERS (IDUs) AND HIV/AIDS

Notwithstanding Fianna Fáil Senator Don Lydon's assertion in
1988, during a Seanad debate on AIDS, that "only sodomites,
drug addicts and promiscuous people are at risk from HIV/
AIDS" (Butler, 2002, p. 183), the reality is that the HIV/AIDS
pandemic is sweeping the world. In its wake, it is bringing devastation and death to whole sections of the population and not
just to the three groups referred to by Lydon. AIDS (acquired
immunodeficiency syndrome) claimed 3.1 million lives in 2002
with a further 5 million contracting HIV (human immunodeficiency virus), bringing to 42 million people the number living
with the virus at the end of 2002 (UNAIDS/WHO, 2002, p. 3).

HIV/AIDS is expanding at an alarming rate in Asia, particularly in China, India and Indonesia, and in the former Soviet
bloc countries. Intravenous drug use is a major contributor to
the spread of HIV/AIDS. It is also one of the most efficient
modes of transmission, even more so than sexual intercourse.

However, it is in Eastern Europe and in Central Asia that the
fastest-growing HIV/AIDS epidemic is to be found. It is also the
only region where intravenous drug use is cited as the main
mode of transmission — in the other seven regions, heterosexual and homosexual intercourse are also cited as modes of

transmission. Kazakhstan, Azerbaijan, Georgia, Kyrgyzstan, Tajikistan and Uzbekistan have all recorded spectacular increases in HIV matched by equally spectacular increases in drug consumption. Uzbekistan in particular is reported as experiencing "an explosive growth" (UNAIDS/WHO, 2002, p. 13) in HIV infections. High numbers of IDU-related HIV cases, in per capita terms, are also reported from the countries in the Baltic region — Latvia, Estonia, Ukraine and Belarus in particular. Estonia has the highest rate of new HIV infection in this region. Lithuania is experiencing a major HIV outbreak in its prisons, where 285 prisoners (15 per cent of the prison population) in one prison contracted HIV. Russia has one of the highest intravenous drug-using populations with HIV in the world. Up to 90 per cent of HIV infection in Russia is as a result of IDU. Given the nature of intravenous drug use, it is difficult to gauge exact figures; however the evidence that exists indicates that IDU-transmitted HIV can increase at a very rapid rate and can quickly feed into the wider population.

That increase is likely to continue into the immediate future, as some IDUs are starting at a very early age — some as young as 13–14 years of age. One study among Moscow secondary-school students revealed that 4 per cent had injected drugs. Yet there is a dearth of knowledge and understanding about the potential deadly affects of HIV/AIDS in these countries amongst the general population. In a study conducted in 2001 in Azerbaijan and Uzbekistan, one-third of young women aged 15–24 had never heard of AIDS (UNAIDS/WHO, 2002, p. 15).

The dramatic increase in drug consumption in these former Soviet Union states coincides with the abrupt and unexpected collapse of the Soviet communist system in 1989. In the fragmentation that followed, social structures shattered and in the headlong rush to embrace capitalism, the majority of people were left behind in grinding poverty, alienated from the new order. One of the consistent outcomes of grinding poverty, rising unemployment, plummeting living standards and the rapid increase in intravenous drug use is that it forces women, and men to a much lesser degree, into prostitution. Prostitution in turn becomes part of the HIV transmission problem. In Russia and the Ukraine, 30 per cent of female IDUs are involved in the sex trade with 13–17 per cent HIV prevalence rates amongst sex workers found in studies conducted in Moscow, St Petersburg and Donetsk (UNAIDS/WHO, 2002, p. 15). The rapid increase in drug consumption and the corresponding increase in HIV will add further to the social and economic woes of these countries.

As many of the HIV-infected people contract full-blown AIDS, the scale of the problems facing these countries will become even more apparent over the next ten years. Given the dire state of many of these economies, the cost of providing for these people will be beyond them. The problem facing Central Asian countries underscores the relationship between poverty, dislocation, alienation and debilitating drug use.

The poverty and underdevelopment that is currently driving HIV and in particular IDU-transmitted HIV in Central Asia is also driving HIV in Latin and Central America. Forced migration to the already overcrowded, unhygienic and poverty-dominated *barrios* and *favelas* (shanty towns) is a major cause of intravenous drug use and resultant high levels of HIV. The risk of the spread of HIV from IDU to other sections of the population is serious. In one study in Rio de Janeiro, 83 per cent of drug users said that they did not use condoms with their regular partners and 63 per cent said that they never used condoms, even with their occasional partners (Regan, 2002, p. 197). The consequent transmission from mothers to babies is very high.

UNAIDS/WHO (2002) report growing concern about the sharing of injecting drug equipment and the consequent rise in rates of HIV infection in Argentina, Brazil, Chile, Paraguay, Uruguay and in parts of Mexico. Apart from the optimism generated by the recent (2002) election of the left-of-centre labour leader Luiz Inácio Da Silva — political ally of Hugo Chavez in Venezuela and Fidel Castro in Cuba — as President of Brazil, there is no immediate prospect in sight that the economic prospects of Latin and Central America will substantially improve. Despite some success as a result of the introduction of harm reduction measures, the immediate prospect for a reduction in the overall level of IDU and consequent spread of HIV seems remote.

Africa remains, however, the continent most at risk from HIV/AIDS and it is also targeted as a growth centre for drug traffickers. Illicit drug use has traditionally been lower in Africa than in other countries. About 2.4 million Africans died from AIDS in 2002 with approximately 3.5 million new infections occurring at the same time. In all, about 29.4 million Africans are living with HIV/AIDS, with 10 million in the 15–24 age group and just under 3 million under the age of 15. The current epidemic in Africa could easily be exasperated by increased drug use and in particular by increased intravenous drug consumption.

Countries in Eastern and Southern Africa have experienced recent increased consumption of opiates, particularly heroin. Kenya, Zambia, Namibia and South Africa have all experienced increases in consumption. Within South Africa, the region of Gauteng, incorporating Johannesburg and Pretoria, along with Cape Town are particularly affected. While overall levels of intravenous drug consumption are much lower in Africa than elsewhere, should that situation change in the future, Africa would be ill-prepared for yet another devastating epidemic.

The situation is not, however, without hope. Countries are beginning to implement strategies that are positively impacting on the prevalence of HIV/AIDS. Harm reduction programmes have been implemented in Argentina, Chile, Brazil, Paraguay and Uruguay. There are some indications that condom use among injecting drug users, while still not sufficiently high, is increasing. There are also hopeful signs from South Africa, Uganda and Ethiopia that intervention programmes are having an effect, particularly among young women. The rate of infection in parts of these countries is beginning to decline for the first time since the disease hit.

Ireland cannot regard itself as exempt from these global patterns. Greater mobility between countries as people move in search of more exotic holiday destinations or in search of work and survival means that the spread of HIV/AIDS infection is very real. To assert this is not to argue for battening down the customs hatches. Such assertions cannot be equated with a call for more draconian laws to stem the trickle of people that make the long journey from poor to rich countries. To assert the danger of the spread of HIV/AIDS is not a call for further ring-fencing of the Western world against those who aspire to what they hope will be a better way of life; nor is it a call for support for more xenophobic policies. Rather it is a call for action to effect change in the unjust social and economic circumstances that result in increase in intravenous drug use and the consequent spread of HIV/AIDS. Whatever answers exist, it is clear that more laws and prisons do not offer any solutions, as the next section will highlight.

PRISONERS AND DRUG USE

Whatever about being an excuse for crime, poverty is certainly an indicator. Bacik et al. confidently declare that the "evidence linking crime and poverty is overwhelming" (1998, p. vi). O'Mahony's (2000) review of prison policy in this country gives further credence to the strong correlation between crime and poverty. Irish prisoners in the main come from socially disadvantaged areas, which is not to suggest that all crime is committed by people from socially disadvantaged areas. O'Mahony claims that the elite is, in some respect, above the law. This view would appear to be vindicated by the decision of a court judge that an unbiased jury could not be found to sit on the trial of former Taoiseach, Charles Haughey, on charges of obstructing a tribunal, thereby ensuring that he never came to trial.

Supporting O'Mahony's assertion that custodial sentencing reflects strong levels of class bias, Bacik et al. (1998) put a precise figure on the level of bias. They estimate that "defendants from the more deprived areas are 49 per cent more likely to receive custodial sentences than those from less deprived areas" (1998, p. 26). Quoting Michel Foucault with approval, O'Mahony states that "the true underlying function of prison is not to control the criminal so much as to control the working class by creating the criminal" (2000, p. 6).

Drug policies in most countries, according to Flynn (2001), are underpinned by the belief that longer prison sentences for drug use will ultimately limit their use. The evidence, at least in relation to the Netherlands and the UK where comparative work has been conducted, does not sustain that view. There is far less use of cannabis in the Netherlands where there are no legal penalties for possession of small amounts for personal use whereas, up to the recent announcements in the UK, there were heavy penalties and much higher levels of consumption.

Between 1996 and January 2000, the numbers imprisoned in England and Wales for drug offences rose from 6,900 to 9,610. Yet there was no corresponding reduction in drug consumption.

There are some state exceptions to the imprisonment culture. Since 1991, Swiss policy has been moving away from a policy of criminalisation towards harm reduction. In 1999, the Swiss Federal Department of Health issued a report arguing that cannabis does relatively little damage to health and that consumption cannot be regulated through prohibition. In 1999, there were 44,336 (Flynn, 2001, p. 11) violations of the 1951 federal law on narcotics. Over 80 per cent of these were for possession or consumption. However, only a small proportion of these were charged or imprisoned.

For those who were imprisoned, Switzerland introduced a needle-exchange programme in 1994 and also pioneered the prescription of heroin to those severely addicted in specialist treatment centres. There are twenty treatment centres offering 1,194 places and in 2000, only 1,038 were occupied (Flynn, 2001, p. 11). The Parliamentary Assembly of the Council of Europe commended "the government of Switzerland for its success in stabilising and then reducing the number of drug-related deaths since 1994" (Flynn, 2001, p. 2).

In preparing the National Drugs Strategy 2001–2008, the Inter-Departmental group that studied policies in other countries reviewed the Swiss approach but did not recommend needle exchange programmes in Ireland. Nelles et al., cited in Dillon, reported that "the experience of the syringe distribution in prison in Switzerland was entirely positive" (Dillon, 2001, p. 133). No security problems were reported and there was no evidence of any increase in prisoner drug use.

In Ireland, however, once in prison, the opportunity for drug use while obviously not as great as it was in the deprived communities, from which many prisoners have come, still exists. That prisons are drug-infested disease-ridden institutions appears to be accepted by the state without due concern. According to the *EMCDDA 2000 Report*, conditions in prisons are even more conducive to the spread of drug-induced infectious disease than conditions outside (2000, p. 27) — a view shared by UNAIDS/WHO. Ireland is not unique in this regard.

> The concentration of large numbers of young people in overcrowded prisons or juvenile justice facilities, often marked by an abundance of drugs but a scarcity of HIV information, clean needles and condoms, provides fertile ground for rapid spread of HIV among inmates and, upon their eventual release, into the wider population. (UNAIDS/WHO, 2002, p. 14)

Mountjoy in particular has a serious heroin problem, tacitly approved of, many prisoners argue, to contain the massive overcrowding in the prison. Lucy Dillon's in-depth study of 29 prisoners in Mountjoy would seem to confirm this perception. Dillon concludes that

> drugs play a complex role in influencing the day-to-day atmosphere within the prison . . . a prison with a number of its population under the influence of drugs was seen to produce a calm atmosphere, when drugs were not available a particularly tense atmosphere was perceived to result. (Dillon, 2001, p. 60)

Dillon quotes from two of the people whom she interviewed as follows: "I think they're happy at certain times that there's drugs in the jail. It keeps a lid on it, it does. I think they let it in." Another prisoner made a similar claim: "It's fucking a lot quieter when there's drugs in the prison 'cause everyone is stoned, but when there's no drugs, there's fighting and a lot of tension in the place."

Drawing on research conducted by the Department of Community Health and General Practice, Trinity College, Dublin (1999), the National Drugs Strategy 2001–2008 reports that 17 per cent started injecting in prison, and 43 per cent share injecting equipment inside prison. Injecting is the preferred means of drug use in prisons despite the short supply of injecting equipment — estimated in Dillon's study at three in the male section — despite the obvious risks from HIV and hepatitis. Injecting is seen to be more direct in its effect and less wasteful of a precious commodity. According to The National Drugs Strategy (2001–2008), prisons in Dublin "have more drug misuse among the prison population and higher rates of infection than any other prisons in the country" (2001, p. 26).

Prisons provide neither respite from the general conditions of poverty and deprivation that the bulk of prisoners experience prior to their incarceration, nor does it necessarily protect them from the realities of drug-domination. That their drug use is linked to their social and economic circumstances is without question. That prison, for many, only exacerbates their difficulties is also without question. Notwithstanding such a scenario, imprisonment for drug-related crime continues to be a favoured option of the State. Despite an actual decrease of crime between 1995 and 1999 of about 20 per cent (O'Mahony, 2000, p. 25), as a society we continue to incarcerate people at an extraordinarily high rate. In essence, the state is creating an environment that not only increases the likelihood of drug use, but also increases the likelihood of the spread of infectious disease.

There have been some efforts at finding alternatives to incarceration. The introduction of Drugs Courts is one innovative and welcome alternative. Presented as the "radical alternative for drug addicts" (*Irish Times* Commercial Supplement, 29 September 2001, p. 13), the new Drug Courts are an attempt to break the cycle of crime and drug use. Currently confined to Dublin's north inner city, this multi-disciplinary pilot initiative involving the Gardaí, medical personnel, the probation service and education personnel oversee offenders in a year-long programme starting with drug stabilisation and ending in employment. Offenders may detox either in their own community or in hospital or they may take a methadone maintenance programme. Central to the programme is a contract between the Court and the offender and team meetings to assess the needs and progress of the participants. Even if offenders break the contract, automatic imprisonment does not follow. However, if there are repeated breaches of contract, the Court can send the offender back to the regular court and imprisonment can follow. Short-term imprisonment can be imposed if the judge so decides.

Clearly people from working-class backgrounds are more likely to go to jail than are their middle-class counterparts. Prison, while ostensibly offering protection to society, offers little to the prisoners. Drugs are part of prison life and inadequate resources are given over to the protection of prisoners' health or enabling them participate in quality programmes that might address the root causes of their imprisonment. Many prisoners are released back into society without any attempt to address their needs, including their addiction needs. In that context, the punitive approach to drug-related crime is not working. The protection offered to society is only temporary and the protection offered to those in prison is negligible. New approaches are needed both for the sake of the prisoners and for society. The Drugs Courts mark an important step in new thinking.

ENVIRONMENTAL FACTORS IN DRUG USE

Broad agreement exists that adverse economic conditions do significantly contribute to drug use. The physical environment can reinforce a sense of self-worth or can have the opposite effect of inducing a sense of defeatism and powerlessness that can be manifested at both the individual and community level. There is a clear correlation between poor quality environment and drug-related problems. Substance abuse in the inner city is "merely a symptom of deeper dynamics of social marginalisation and alienation" (Bourgois, 1995, p. 2).

James Q. Wilson uses the image of the broken window in Kelling and Coles (1996) to illustrate how an area can degenerate and how the accumulation of that degeneration can have a demoralising effect on the residents:

> We use the image of broken windows to explain how neighbourhoods may decay into disorder and even crime if no one attends faithfully to their maintenance. If a factory or office window is broken, passers-by observing it will conclude that no one cares or no one is in charge. In time a few will begin throwing stones to break more windows. Soon all windows will be broken and now passers by will think that, not only is no one in charge of the building, no one is in charge of the street on which it faces. Only the young, the criminal or the foolhardy have any business on an unprotected avenue and so more and more citizens will begin to abandon the street to those they assume prowl it. Small dis-

orders lead to larger and larger ones. (Kelling and Coles, 1996, p. *xv*)

Kelling and Coles cite the experiences of New Haven, Chicago, New York, Indianapolis and Milwaukee residents who identified abandoned cars and graffiti as major problems ahead of issues like public drunkenness, street prostitution and youth gangs. Three out of five people in New York say dirt, graffiti and noise have reduced their quality of life before going on to list panhandlers, homeless people and beggars. Concern was also expressed about damage to public spaces such as bus shelters, street signs and the accumulation of rubbish. In such settings, anti-social behaviour increases, drug-related problems increase and become more visible, community morale is lessened, property prices collapse, people move out, inward investment is non-existent and crime thrives.

They cite the experience of Baltimore as evidence of an abandoned city that reclaimed itself. In January 1993, after a prolonged period of increasing violence and unprecedented levels of murder, the mayor and community-based organisations (those that still existed) decided to act. Their first priority was to address the level of physical decay in the area. Abandoned houses were the first targets. These were either boarded up or in some cases demolished. They fenced off or closed walkways between houses that had become no-go areas, cleaned up the rubbish, turned waste-ground into community gardens, took court-action against what they regarded as irresponsible landlords in the area. Foot-patrols by the police were reintroduced. The result of this concerted effort was the reduction in crime levels by 56 per cent over a two-year period.

Such concerns are not just to be found in the United States. In an unpublished study conducted in this country one community activist in a deprived urban area identified broken glass as the single biggest problem in the area. This, she said, restricted children's play areas and caused serious accidents and was a source of infection.

The case for environmental action and for healthy environments is not confined to how it will impact of drug use. A good quality ecologically sustainable environment should be a right for all citizens, irrespective of income levels or social class. Environmental revival is not in itself the only solution to inner city decay. It is not, in the words of one person living in an inner city area, as if sticking in flowerpots all over the place is the answer to everything.

While a sticking plaster approach will not contribute in any substantial way to sustainable development, environmental regeneration in an ecologically sustainable setting is but one of a number of key interventions required in addressing poverty, alienation, drug use and general disaffection and malaise.

SUMMARY

This chapter has attempted to promote a deeper understanding of how the debate on drugs impinges on and is influenced by a whole range of other issues, not least how people perceive drug users. Race and racial stereotyping has become inextricably linked to the criminalisation of certain drugs. Dating back to the early part of the last century, the campaign for the criminalisation of drugs was linked to fear of dilution of racial purity as a result of miscegenation. White fear of racial contact with mainly Black people did not inhibit the White-dominated medical profession from testing drugs on Black and Hispanic people. It does not discourage western pharmaceutical companies from trying to increase profits from sales of what some commentators regard as sub-standard products to the continents of origin of Afro-Americans and Hispanics.

The discussion also points to evidence suggesting strong class and age bias in the way drug use is problematised. Despite relatively high levels of use among university students, and young professionals, there appears to be less focus and less concern about their level of use. Working class users are much more likely to be imprisoned than are their middle-class counterparts. For different reasons, there also appears to be less focus and less awareness of the distinctive aspects of drug use among ethnic minorities.

Drug use amongst Ireland's largest ethnic minority, the Travelling community, is different in a number of respects from that of settled people. Whether the pattern of consumption that exists amongst members of the Travelling community differs significantly from other minority ethnic groups is yet to be established. Older people's drug use seems not only to be openly tolerated but actively encouraged by the medical profession and the pharmaceutical companies.

Clear differences also emerged in the review of the literature on the impact of drug use on women and men and on the gay community. One commentator took the benign view that women's drug use was an expression of their freedom and capacity to generate pleasure for themselves. Others take the opposite view that drug use is further evidence of exploitation by patriarchal structures albeit patriarchal structures of the street rather than the institution. The review also clearly highlighted the extent to which intravenous drug use contributes to the spread of HIV/AIDS and in particular highlighted the way this is happening in the former Soviet Union bloc countries of Central Asia. The chapter also examined the environmental context that can significantly contribute to an overall sense of malaise in a community that can then have knock-on effects on drug use.

Chapter 4

STRATEGIES AND INTERVENTIONS

INTRODUCTION

As outlined in Chapter One, there is a strong history of prevention paralleling traditionally high levels of alcohol consumption in Ireland. While the concept of prevention is often presented as non-problematic, Morgan (2001) argues that it is in fact plagued with imprecision and lack of clarity. Harm reduction, on the other hand, is generally regarded as less amenable to pithy definition. Notwithstanding the ambiguity that often surrounds the concept, it has become an integral part of the drug lexicon. Other terms used in conjunction with harm reduction include "responsible drug use", "secondary provision", "nuisance reduction", "casualty-reduction" and "risk management". "Manageability" of the drug problem, according to Dorn and Lee (1999, p. 97), has replaced the "more heroic but politically acceptable war stance", a stance outlined in Chapter Two. How to respond poses a real dilemma for policy makers and practitioners.

This chapter will review a range of different approaches to tackling drug-related problems and will present these approaches in the context of prevention and harm reduction. The following questions will be addressed in this chapter.

- What is generally understood by the terms harm reduction and prevention?

- Can the different approaches that have been put in place either in this country or internationally be characterised either as prevention or harm reduction initiatives?

HARM REDUCTION — AN OVERVIEW

The essence of harm reduction, according to Riley and O'Hare (2000, p. 6), is reflected in the following statement:

> If a person is not willing to give up his or her drug use, we should assist them in reducing harm to him or herself or others.

It is essentially a pragmatic policy aimed at minimising the damage that drug users do to themselves, their family, friends and their local community. There are no clear-cut answers in harm reduction. Not only are there no clear-cut answers within the harm-reduction paradigm, there are also no clear-cut measurements that might provide those answers. Flynn (2001) states that "it is worth noting, however, that there are no rigorously defined and generally accepted criteria for measuring drug-related harm" (2001, p 4). It recognises that drug use is a complex phenomenon that at its worst is a chronic relapsing condition that is not responsive to simplistic solutions.

There is some disagreement as to the origins of the term. Inciardi and Harrison (2000, p. *viii*) argue that it originated in 1984 with needle exchange programmes in the Netherlands with the aim of stemming the number of hepatitis cases related to drug use, while others (Rhodes and Stimson, 1998, p. 159) argue that it originated in Australia. In response to the HIV/AIDS crisis, harm reduction grew in popularity and became part of the drug policies of many countries. In Ireland, the methadone programme is probably the best-known example of harm reduction where one perceived less harmful drug (methadone) is provided to heroin (a harmful drug) addicts who are either unwilling or unable to kick their heroin habit.

For the advocates of harm reduction, the key to success is the degree to which the intervention has not further isolated, ostracised or demonised the drug user. Harm reduction programmes like the one in Merseyside in the 1980s involved a range of agencies from housing to employment, health care, education and training as well as the type of exchange programmes outlined above. In addition, the Merseyside project included personal contact, counselling when sought by the users and some form of tracking that did not involve surveillance of users. The rights of the individual and an acceptance that drug use is here to stay underpin the harm reduction approach.

According to Riley and O'Hare (2000, p. 6), the main characteristics of harm reduction are:

- Pragmatism

- Humanistic values — no moralistic judgement is made to either condemn or support drug use

- Focus on the harm — the harms addressed can be related to health, social, economic or a multitude of other factors affecting the individual, community and society as a whole.

For Inciardi and Harrison (2000, p. *xi*) the following questions are central to harm reduction:

- How can we reduce the likelihood that drug users will engage in criminal and other undesirable activities?

- How can we reduce overdoses, HIV/AIDS and the hepatitis B and C infections associated with the use of some drugs?

- How can we increase the chances that drug users will act responsibly towards others?

- How can we increase the likelihood of rehabilitation?

- More generally, how do we ensure that drug control policies do not cause more harm to drug users and society than drug use itself?

Korf and Buning (2000, p. 132) broadly agree with all of the above but add what is probably one significant extra component — optimism.

The following applications are just some examples of harm reduction strategies/goals:

- Substitution treatment programmes like methadone;

- Needle exchange programmes for drug users both inside and outside of prison;

- The provision of injecting/consumption rooms;

- Provision of disinfectants;

- Arrest referral schemes and the use of Drug Courts;

- Decriminalising of small scale drug offences;

- Pre-release and aftercare for prisoners;

- Safer dancing guidelines.

Harm reduction is viewed as both a goal and a strategy. The term harm reduction also brings into focus what is meant by the word "harm". Kiely and Egan (2000, p. 8) argue that initial understandings of the word harm were very narrow, referring only to the individual user. Drug-related harm causes varying levels of difficulty for individuals, families, communities and society. In setting the goal or agreeing the strategy of harm reduction, the question of whose harm is central.

The development of relevant harm reduction strategies/ goals can only be effective if they take into account the particular drug problem in its localised setting. What separates this approach/goal from other approaches is the recognition that the notion of a "drug-free" society is unattainable. This recognition is, for many, a step too far, an ideological chasm that they are unable to overcome.

Merchants Quay Ireland operates the best-known harm reduction initiative in this country. Established in 1989 by the Franciscan Community in response to an increase in the number of drug users seeking help within the locality, the preferred model concentrates on reducing or eliminating risks, insofar as that is possible, among a population many of whom engage in high-risk injecting and sexual behaviour. Merchants Quay Ireland works in partnership with a wide variety of both statutory and voluntary agencies to provide a comprehensive array of services for drug users and for families and communities affected by drugs.

In 1992, the Project established a Health Promotion Unit and an evaluation (Cox and Lawless, 2000) indicated that the Unit was highly successful in making initial contact with injecting drug users, attracting women and girl drug users, and attracting those involved in high-risk behaviour. The report favourably commented on the needle exchange programme and among other things recommended access to sterile injecting equipment at a local and community level.

Many of the objectives of the Unit are directed at changing the drug-using behaviour of the people who access their services. Specifically, the objectives include reducing the use of risky combinations of drugs and reducing the frequency of use. In short, all behaviour change in the direction of reduced or safer use, no matter how insignificant, is regarded as valuable progress. These safer practices include how to inject more safely, the importance of cleaning prior to injecting, the use of swabs and the encouragement of independent injecting.

Commenting on the Project in the 1999 Annual Report, Gerry Raftery OFM, the Justice Director, writes as follows:

> It requires hospitality, patience, acceptance and a readiness to recognise the innate dignity of each person no matter how terrible their circumstances. The project stays with people in their chaos in the knowledge that we will also be with them when they come to their senses. (Merchant's Quay, 1999, p. 2)

While policy-makers and users in the developed world grapple with the implications of their understandings and perceived consequences of harm reduction, equally people in the developing world, as briefly mentioned above, are grappling with the concept both from the perspective of the consumer and from the perspective of the producer. The similarity of issues is quite striking.

Calls for decriminalisation of cultivation for subsistence quantities in the so-called "developing" world are matched with calls for decriminalisation of possession of small quantities for personal use in the so-called "developed" world. Equally, calls for specific measures to enhance the level of health and well-being of producers through the prevention of environmental pollution related to the handling of pesticides and chemicals at farm level and from aerial bombardment are matched with calls for specific measures to enhance the health and well-being of consumers through the provision of clean needles, injecting rooms, methadone as well as proper treat- ment and social welfare provision.

As in the majority developed world, non-governmental organisations in the minority developing world have led the move
away from punitive to more community-based, person-centred
policies. But if these approaches are to succeed they must address the ever-pressing macroeconomic forces that drive people
into large-scale production and unhealthy levels of consumption.

One of the main objections put forward in opposition to
harm reduction, at the consumption end of the spectrum, is
based on a kind of idealism that believes that young people are
being badly served by the concept of less harm. The objective,
they argue, should be to prevent any harm at all. In defence of
harm reduction, Riley and O'Hare claim that harm reduction is
"concerned with ensuring the quality and integrity of human
life in all of its wonderful, awful complexity" (2000, p. 23).

PREVENTION

Drug prevention has become an umbrella term encompassing a
range of interventions with specific aims, objectives and meth-
odologies. Along with supply reduction, treatment and research, prevention is one of the four pillars of the government's
response to the drug "problem" in Ireland as outlined in the
National Drugs Strategy 2001–2008. The Departments of Health
and Children and Education and Science are identified in the
National Drugs Strategy as having direct responsibility for
promoting prevention. The involvement of the Department of
Education and Science highlights the linkage between drug
prevention and educational disadvantage.

Uhl, cited in Morgan (2001), has attempted to assimilate the
main features of prevention and in the process distinguishes
between primary prevention, secondary prevention, tertiary
prevention (Type A) and tertiary prevention (Type B). Each is
described as follows:

- Primary prevention is to prevent the onset of a substance-
  related problem.

- Secondary prevention is to intervene if a problem is likely to
  occur (prevention in high risks groups) or if a problem exists but is not yet fully manifested.

- Tertiary prevention (Type A) involves dealing with problems once they are fully manifested (prevention of further harm in those addicted).

- Tertiary prevention (Type B) involves prevention of further problems recurring once they have successfully been treated (relapse prevention) (Morgan, 2001, pp. 13–14).

These definitions of prevention highlight the overlap that exists between definitions of prevention and harm reduction; the term "prevention of further harm" — essentially harm reduction — is even used in these definitions. Clear blue water does not exist between these concepts. Notwithstanding the blurring of distinctions in Uhl's classification, there is at least in popular perception an equating of prevention with abstinence. Given that association, both prevention and abstinence are used interchangeably here.

Schools and youth groups are perceived to be the most effective, though not the only location for communicating the prevention message. The terms "drug prevention" and "drug education" are often used interchangeably but education *per se* need not have a preventative focus. Many education programmes operate the choice model, with the intention of enabling young people to make informed choices. Whether it is possible or even desirable to adopt a strictly neutral position is a moot point. It would appear that in this area, as in others, it is not possible.

Internationally, hundreds of millions of pounds have been spent on drugs education and drug prevention programmes. In the view of Carlen and Morgan (1999, p. 162), there is very little to show for the investment. Plant et al. (1985) agree with the limits of educational programmes to bring about any significant drop in the use of drugs. They argue that despite the considerable sums of money that continue to be spent and the proliferation of agencies involved, "most of the evidence related to results is depressing". By 1992, Plant and Plant had become more convinced about the inability of the educational system to effect change in the pattern of drug consumption. "Sadly," they conclude, "available evidence on the effectiveness of post alcohol and drug use makes depressing reading" (1992, p. 124). No known method of drug education can be said to reduce drug use. This "sombre view", they say, is supported by extensive research.

EDUCATIONAL INTERVENTIONS

Education continues to be presented as the panacea for all ills — "if it's broken, education will fix it" would appear to be the motto. The present curricular overload is testimony to the belief that education can seriously impact on the behaviour and attitudes of young people. For all the emphasis that is put on education, and for all the problems that are laid at its door, the capacity of education to respond to all of these demands is strongly contested. Fullan and Stiegelbaur (1992) paint a rather bleak picture of educational innovation and specific programme interventions declaring that there is "much faddism, superficiality, confusion and failure, too many competing demands or overload, underfunding of projects and trying too much with too little" (1992, p. 4) to effect serious change.

What we need, according to Fullan and Stiegelbaur (1992), is to create a more coherent picture of the process of educational change and a greater understanding of the roles of those who are involved in that change. While the dynamic that affects the process of educational change is too complex to deal with here, it would appear from the literature that the essence of educational change consists in learning new ways of thinking and doing, new skills, knowledge and attitudes. Changing the culture of institutions and the people who work in them is the real agenda. For change to work it must be meaningful and real.

The out-of-school environment also affects serious change and this can be crucially important either as a catalyst for or a brake on change. The educational system and schools are particularly susceptible to outside powers and to being influenced by particular pressure groups. O'Reilly (undated) chronicles how various pressure groups in the Republic of Ireland successfully organised and pressurised for change or to resist particular kinds of change in social policy in the 1970s, 1980s and 1990s — pressure that directly impacted on school policy.

The introduction of SPHE — the curricular area under which drug education comes in this country — and RSE programmes in the Republic of Ireland have been strongly influenced by broader socio-religious-political factors (Inglis, 1998; Mac an Ghaill et al., 2002). Their successful dissemination can — at least in the short term — be radically influenced by small vocal interest groups. External factors are hugely influential in understanding the process of curricular change and in particular in situations where dominant interests are perceived to be under threat.

Implementing change for specific outcomes is not an easy task. In their introduction to the review of the effectiveness of *On My Own Two Feet*, a government-funded second-level drug education programme, Morgan et al. (1996) conclude that it is difficult to get health-related messages across to young people. Even when it is attempted, the message tends to impact more on attitudes and beliefs rather than actual behaviour.

Despite this pessimistic assessment, innovation and change in the Irish educational system has not lost its appeal. Recent interventions in the curriculum have sought to promote civic, social and political awareness and responsibility. Environmental awareness, personal health and sexual programmes have also been introduced. Short-term programmes have been introduced to promote awareness of HIV/AIDS and two programmes, *Walk Tall* and *On My Own Two Feet*, exist at both first and second level to address the drugs issue.

The Green Paper *Education for a Changing World* (1992) sought in co-operation with the Department of Health to "develop a model for implementing effective substance abuse education within the context of health education in schools" (1992, p. 132). The White Paper *Charting our Education Future* (1995) committed the Department to the "development of programmes relating to tobacco, alcohol and substance abuse and the promotion of a healthy lifestyle" (1995, p. 163).

That the Irish government should look to education is in keeping with other governments in the western world who want to intervene and reduce, if not eliminate, the use of drugs in society. The National Drugs Strategy 2001–2008 seeks to "strengthen resilience amongst young people in or out of school by fostering positive stable relationships with family or key community figures especially in the early years" (2001, p. 98).

However, neither the Green nor White Papers grappled with the more difficult and potentially controversial task of *how* these programmes were to be developed and *what* message was to be central to them. Clearly, there is resistance to harm reduction approaches being adopted in schools. The feel-good "say no to drugs" model will always find favour with some people, lest any compromise would result in the opening of the floodgates. Right across Europe and in the United States, governments have sought ways in which a simple prevention message can be communicated in schools and other educational centres. In addition to these, a range of initiatives have also been developed in what has become known as the non-formal sector. Given the plethora of these interventions in both formal and non-formal areas of learning — according to the EMCDDA (2001), there are 53 different programmes within the EU alone — it is beyond the scope of this work to review each and every one. Fourteen have been selected as examples of the kind of interventions that are taking place.

MODELS OF INTERVENTION USING THE HARM REDUCTION/ PREVENTION-ABSTINENCE MODEL

Fourteen interventions are detailed below using the above framework. These interventions can best be represented as continuums rather than dichotomous entities although it is clear, at least with regard to the intention of some of the promoters, that a prevention/abstinence outcome rather than a harm reduction outcome would result. For example, the police-run programmes, particularly the DARE programme in the United States, were specifically designed to prevent and promote abstinence and eschew harm reduction strategies. The same tends to apply to public information campaigns, although that may be about to change. The opposite is not necessarily the case.

Harm reduction advocates do not necessarily shun prevention/abstinence as it could be argued that prevention/abstinence is the ultimate harm reduction. A managing risk programme clearly comes within the harm reduction paradigm, whereas the Social Skills Training could conceivably reflect both typologies. However, some programmes are primarily focused or lean more in the direction of one rather than the other. The decision on where to locate each of the interventions detailed below is very much subjective.

Morgan et al. (1996) argue that there are essentially three approaches or models. The first of these involves the presentation of facts on drugs — this is not an unproblematic issue, as will be discussed in more detail below — in the hope that young people will come to the right conclusion, namely to avoid drugs. The second approach involves equipping young people with the skills of withstanding peer pressure to experiment and engage in high-risk behaviour. The final approach involves facilitating young people to make their own decisions, again in the hope/ expectation that they will reject drugs. These particular approaches or models can be discerned in the examples of interventions details below.

Models are by their nature only convenient representations of what are often complex undertakings. Inevitably, the simplifications involved in presenting how particular interventions work are reductionist in nature. Models are also fluid and easily embrace other models and approaches in their implementation. For all these reservations, models retain their usefulness in trying to understand and represent the essences of particular approaches to drug education.

The fourteen interventions that are outlined below are not presented as stand-alone mutually exclusive approaches. Nor are the fourteen interventions to be considered as the definitive statement on the full range of drug interventions within the harm reduction/prevention-abstinence framework. Rather they are presented as examples of interventions that highlight various issues of relevance to drug interventions.

DARE

DARE (Drug Abuse Resistance Education) is currently found in more than half of all school districts in the United States and reaches 25 million students each year. It began in Los Angeles in 1983–84 as a school-based drug prevention programme. Taught by police officers who receive 80 hours training, it is popular with teachers, the police, school managers, parents, policy makers and politicians. Endorsed by both Bill Clinton and George W. Bush, the programme receives huge federal funding.

Clayton et al. (1996, p. 96) believe that DARE is popular with the teachers because it gives them respite from teaching in the classroom and allows them to shed responsibility (presuming one accepts that it is part of their responsibility in the first place) for teaching this lifeskill (again presuming one accepts that drug education is a lifeskill). It is popular with principals/managers because police presence, many principals/managers believe, increases in-school security in an increasingly volatile setting. It is popular with the police because it gives them access to the schools and enables them to fulfil their community-policing mandate. It is popular with parents who are concerned with the increasing threat not only of drug use but of in-school violence.

The aim of the programme is to prevent substance abuse among school children. Its approach is based on police officers' accounts of dealing in the street or in local neighbourhoods with seriously addicted people and the consequences for their lives and for their families.

Analysing the programme, Clayton et al. (1996, p. 102) are very dismissive of its impact, arguing that the programme finds support because it satisfies all the actors apart from the target group, who remain "stubbornly indifferent to its message". Not only that, Clayton et al. found that drug use (marijuana, inhalants, LSD, stimulants and cigarettes) all began to rise significantly among the cohort (8th, 10th, and 12th graders) at which the programme was aimed. The 2002 UNODCCP report would give further credence to Clayton's assertions. According to this report, results from school surveys — which the Report concludes are more reliable than other surveys, most notably household surveys — indicate that "12th graders those aged seventeen and a few aged eighteen have annual prevalence rates four times the general population average" (UNODCCP, 2002, p. 214).

The programmes did not even have the spin-off effect of promoting good relationships with the police. Clayton et al. (1996) argue that it is naïve to think that one centrally devised and pre-planned programme can meaningfully accommodate all kinds of learners in all kinds of schools and could exert enough influence to counter the forces driving youth towards experimentation with drugs.

The contracting of drug education to outside agencies is strongly criticised by Cohen (1996) cited in Kiely and Egan (2000, p. 10). He argues that contracting out the job of drug education sensationalises the issue and undermines the role of teachers. If teachers, he rhetorically asks, are capable of teaching about the First World War — an event outside of their own experience — surely they are capable, given some specific training, of teaching about drugs.

Bringing outsiders such as police officers, medical professionals, former addicts, addiction counsellors and community activists into the classroom and giving them *sole* responsibility for such programmes invariably results in an uneven, uncoordinated and perhaps even a narrow or subjective account of the whole issue. While these people have particular insights, they do not necessarily have the pedagogical skills to sensitively address the issue. Current educational practice, far from excluding a role for outside interventions and visitors to the classroom, actively encourages it, but believe that they are only effective if they are part of an overall programme that is managed and taught by the teacher and reflects a whole school policy.

Despite the evidence, both the US congress and the federal government have continued to fund programmes that have a drug-free focus and have refused to fund any programmes with a harm reduction focus, despite what Klingemann and Hunt (1998, p. 15) describe as the "mounting evidence in favour of these programmes". The DARE programme continues to find favour with US authorities.

KAB

Similar in many respects to the DARE approach, KAB is an acronym for knowledge, attitude and behaviour. Knowledge, according to this model, influences attitude and attitude influences behaviour. However, knowledge never comes in a value-free way. As outlined earlier, all language is value-laden. In so far as one can have a *pure* model, balanced scientific knowledge is presented about drugs and their effects. The notion that scientific knowledge is *pure* and value-neutral is of course seriously problematic, if not illusory. Programmes may include information on the chemical names of drugs and their pharmacology, the slang names, methods of drug use, the physical and psychological effects including the desirable and undesirable effects.

According to Kiely and Egan (2000, p. 15), the KAB model is based on the "free informed choice" theory, although in reality the model was often located in the preventative/abstinence framework. So while the students were being encouraged to make free informed choices, in reality the expectation was that the choice would result in the rejection of drugs. Initially, the knowledge component was heavily laden with fear. Horror stories of addiction and of personal, physical, psychological, social and moral degeneration were all considered justifiable if they achieved the goal of scaring people into abstinence from illegal drug use. Such tactics are not only ineffective and counterproductive but more seriously undermine the veracity of more measured and credible messages.

And credibility is a key factor — not just the credibility of the message but also of the messenger. Nowlis (1976) cited in Kiely and Egan (2000) asserts that once credibility has been lost, the task of getting an accurate message across becomes all the more difficult.

> Untruths, half-truths, exaggeration, overgeneralization and sensationalism kill credibility. What is said must bear some relationship to what is experienced by the great majority of users. Once credibility is breached, it crumbles like a dam and generalised doubt and distrust remain. (Kiely and Egan, 2000, p. 41)

The belief that police, teachers, parents and others hold special credibility with young people is not supported by evidence. A recent study by the Association of Chief Police Officers, London quoted in *Drug Education Matters* (Spring, 2001), questioned the value of police visitors as drug educators. The report does not suggest that police should be excluded from the classroom but that they should be part of a multi-agency partnership.

In the same way in which the response to the DARE project was negative, the response to KAB has been consistently negative. Among other factors, it has been found that increase in knowledge has no impact on either attitude or behaviour. Plant and Plant (1992, p. 125) and Davenport-Hines (2001, p. 397) are even more emphatic in rejecting the scare tactic approach. Available evidence, argue Plant and Plant, supports the view that "the use of horror approaches is clearly unproductive and should at all costs be avoided". Supporting this view, De Haes and Schuurman (cited in Kiely and Egan, 2000, p. 39) found that students who received a programme of information (either fear arousal or drug facts) were "more likely to have experimented with drugs three months later than students who received no drug education".

Decision-making Model

Essentially, this is a non-directive, non-didactic approach to drug education that facilitates young people to make up their own minds regarding whether or not to use drugs within their overall value system. According to Morgan et al. (1996), young people are given space and opportunity to "ask of themselves whether certain behaviours, i.e. trying out drugs, are consistent with a variety of beliefs and values which they themselves regard as important" (Morgan et al., 1996, p. 8).

The emphasis on personal values is very much part of other models detailed below. It certainly makes a valuable contribution to the Comprehensive Personal and Social Skills Training Approach. There is some evidence, according to Morgan et al. (1996), that this approach works better with older teenagers. A review by Hansen (1992) suggests that "the decision-making approach can make a valuable contribution to the design of a successful programme in the context of other components like social skills" (cited in Morgan et al., 1996, p. 8).

Peer Education

A strong correlation exists between peer influence, low academic achievement and detachment from parent and adult society and values. There is considerable evidence that "having friends, especially close friends who use particular substances and who do not disapprove of the use of these substances is associated with increased likelihood of reported substance use" (Morgan, 2001, p. 20). However there is a chicken-and-egg dimension to peer influence. While peers may be an influence in initiation into drug use, they may also only come into the frame after an individual has started experimentation and then graduates towards other users.

Not surprisingly, given the perceived predominance of peer influence as the starting point for experimentation, education seeks to use that influence to counterbalance what are perceived as negative influences. Peer education has recently come to the fore as an in-school strategy not only in addressing the drug issue but also in combating bullying. The Department of Education and Science *Exploring Masculinities* Programme (2000) advocates peer education as a possible way of tackling bullying in school. The approach works as follows:

> The older pupils act as a support to the younger ones and also provide a line of communication between the teachers and the pupils. The scheme is voluntary and older students are interviewed before they get involved in it. A group of about six senior students is allocated to each class. They are introduced to each other and the scheme is explained. The senior students meet regularly with the co-ordinating teacher and any issue can be raised about the scheme. (Department of Education and Science, 2000, p. 113)

Drug peer education strategy works in a similar way. There are two components to this approach:

1. The presentation of factual, accurate, credible information

2. Peer support for both users and non-users.

When a project decides to adopt this approach, the selection of older students is critically important, including how the younger students perceive them. Typically, although not universally, students who are popular and highly regarded by teachers may not have the "street cred" demanded of younger students who may be experimenting with drugs. Such street cred is often only earned on the street as a user and for obvious reasons users are not good role models for discouraging other young people's drug use. Furthermore, in the selection process, teachers may select students from a more middle-class background as these are very often the students to whom teachers can best relate. These may not find acceptance from the target group.

In reviewing peer-led education approaches, Orlandi (1999, p. 90) identifies the following disadvantages:

- Peer leaders do not have experience in teaching or in classroom management

- Peer leadership requires considerable time and effort in terms of training, co-ordination and scheduling.

She argues that a combination of teacher/peer educators may be the middle ground that can effect change in behaviour and attitude. The teachers can provide the classroom management experience and the youth leadership can facilitate discussion, demonstrating refusal techniques and role-plays. Orlandi does not allude to the issue of the pressure peer educators can be subjected to and how their role as peer leaders can impact on their overall relationship with their own age group. It is very questionable practice to ask young people to take on the responsibility of educating their peers.

Not enough research has been conducted on this approach to warrant any definitive statement of its effectiveness, notwithstanding the reported effectiveness of peer education in combating bullying as outlined in the *Exploring Masculinities* programme. In respect of the peer anti-bullying initiative, in-school research in one Dublin school — quoted in the *Exploring Masculinities* programme — indicates that it has a lot of merit. When first-year students were asked what they thought of the initiative, they were very positive. However, the two peer-led programmes are quite different. The anti-bullying programme operates on a one-to-one and works on a confidentiality basis.

Early indications of peer education drug programmes suggest that young girls may be more influenced by peer-led resistance programmes than young boys. In addition to school-based education, there is a community-based peer education/contact approach. Some serious users/addicts are beyond the reach of practically all social service providers. By their nature, they are difficult to reach, suspicious of professionals, institutions and what they perceive as authority figures. Peer education programmes aim at making contact, however superficial, with these people through their peers by, for example, bringing them into contact with needle exchange programmes and condom use programmes. Ultimately, it operates on the assumption that short-term care can be provided at this remove and that the long-term building of some kind of a bridge between the service provider and the user/addict will bring the two into face-to-face contact. The British *Smack in the Eye* comic is a good example of this kind of education. Circulated by users to users, they are designed to promote safer sex and safer drug use in a high-risk population.

Lucy Dillon (2001, pp. 10, 140) sees potential for in-prison peer education programmes. Peer networks are, she argues, well established and these could be used to educate prisoners about sharing equipment and the risks involved.

As an approach, peer education amongst adults appears to have much to recommend it. It enables hard-to-reach groups to gain access to valuable information and in general from sources that they can trust. Peer education can also overcome language and cultural barriers, as well as location barriers. Education is not location-specific and the learner has control over the learning. It is not necessarily tied to a particular set of values; rather it works best when it addresses specific needs and concerns of the drug user. Adult peer education programmes, be they in the formal sector (e.g. prisons and treatment centres), or the non-formal sector (e.g. the street or homes of users), would appear to have fewer pitfalls than peer education programmes involving teenagers. Peer education at the latter level is more problematic. It may be unfair to ask young people to take on that level of responsibility at this age and may put too much stress on adolescents.

Comprehensive Personal and Social Skills Training

The *Walk Tall* and *On My Own Two Feet* programmes are based on what is referred to as the "Comprehensive Personal and Social Skills Training" approach. This approach recognises that drug use is part of the culture in which we live, is skill-based, combines several approaches to learning and takes account of good pedagogical practice. The *Walk Tall* Programme for primary schools was launched in 1996 has three main strands:

- A substance misuse awareness programme for students, parents and teachers;

- The development of education resource materials and in-service training for teachers;

- Targeting schools where there is a noticeable incidence of substance abuse, particularly heroin (National Drugs Strategy 2001–2008, p. 55).

The main aims of the programme as described in the National Drugs Strategy 2001–2008 are as follows:

- To give students the confidence, skills and knowledge to make healthy choices;

- To seek to avert or delay experimentation;

- To reduce the demand for legal and illegal drugs (National Drugs Strategy, 2001, p. 55).

The post-primary Junior Cycle programme *On My Own Two Feet* was introduced in 1995. The approach is similar to the primary school programme. As part of its Action Plan, the National Drugs Strategy 2001–2008 aimed to implement both programmes in all schools in the Local Drugs Task Force (LDTF) areas in the context of the *Social, Personal, Health Education* (SPHE) programme during the academic year 2001/2002. According to the National Co-ordinator of SPHE Support Services, a regional development officer was appointed by the Department of Education and Science to work specifically with LDTF schools and SPHE was being offered to 80 per cent of all schools by the end of March 2003. Implementation of SPHE will be mandatory in all schools from September 2003.

According to Morgan et al. (1996) the *On My Own Two Feet* programme "does not rely exclusively on any single model of intervention but rather draws on each in an effort to maximise the potential of each one" (Morgan et al., p. 9). There are five major parts to the programme:

- Identity and self-esteem

- Understanding influences

- Assertive communication

- Feelings

- Decision-making (Morgan et al., pp. 8–9).

Morgan et al. (1996) and Morgan (2001) report a number of key findings from their evaluation of *On My Own Two Feet*. The evaluation contrasted students who participated in the programme (the pilot group) with a group of students who did not participate in the programme (the control group). Comparing the study group with the control group, the findings for those that participated in *On My Own Two Feet* are summarised as follows:

- The programme had a significant effect on several key aspects of belief and attitude relevant to substance abuse, particularly alcohol.

- Effects on behaviour were less obvious.

- There were higher scores for self-esteem.

- They were less likely to believe that there were positive consequences to drinking and their attitudes to alcohol were less favourable.

- There were no significant differences to consumption of cigarettes or illegal substance use (Morgan et al., 1996, pp. 16–17).

This programme was also very well received by teachers.

Tobler (1992), cited in Kiely and Egan (2000, p. 63), while agreeing that broad-based skills programmes do have a positive impact, cautions that "school-based programmes will have little carry over unless the community norms support the principles presented by the programme".

The European Monitoring Centre for Drugs and Drug Addiction (EMCDDA) conducted a review of all 53 school-based programmes recorded in their database (EMCDDA, July–August 2001, p. 3). The "life-skill" model is the most used throughout the EU. However, the report goes on to say that this approach is seldom used as a stand-alone. Rather, it is combined with drug knowledge approaches or peer education approaches.

Community-based Interventions

In the view of the (UK) Standing Conference on Drug Abuse (1999, p. 1), "it has long been recognised that there is no single approach to effective drug education and prevention and that the work is the domain of no single agency". In short, the school on its own will never be able to successfully impact on the issue. It has become increasingly apparent that prevention approaches "need to be multi-component and comprehensive and that those based on narrower conceptual frameworks will increasingly fail to address causal factors". Agreeing with the need for a multi-agency, multi-disciplinary response, Brook and Brook (1996, p. 40) argue that programmes that target the individual's interaction with their environment are more likely to be effective. The socio-cultural context in which drug users find themselves is important, they argue.

In his review of the research on community-based interventions, Morgan (2001) divides these interventions into two categories. The first he describes as top-down and as examples he includes:

- Mass media campaigns
- Health warning labels
- Family interventions
- Large-scale community programmes, like the five-year programme in Kansas and Indianapolis in the US, which centred on a school programme, a parents' programme, mass media advertising, community organisation and policies that sought to restrict access and availability.

In terms of bottom-up approaches, he cites the following:

- Empowerment programmes
- Community development
- Multi-sectoral working.

Overall, Morgan (2001) is optimistic about a heterogeneous community-based approach while acknowledging that individual constituent elements on their own are less effective. Much has yet to be learned about the effectiveness of this approach and much research remains to be done.

Alternative Activity Approaches

These programmes are funded by the National Drugs Strategy. Often referred to in the Irish context as "youth diversion" approaches, the emphasis is on organising activities for young people with a view to creating a natural "high" or filling their time creatively and purposefully. Alternative activities require:

- Friendly location for informal activities
- Organised groups to facilitate informal activities
- Night-time activities
- Relevant programmes
- Access to facilities in the area, e.g. swimming pools and sports halls
- Collaborative engagement with other voluntary and statutory bodies in the area.

Alternative activities include either once-off or more sustained medium- to long-term activities. Once-off activities pose a number of questions:

- How are young people selected to participate on these activities?
- Can activities built around events and not processes ensure that relationships can be formed and maintained?

- The indications are that boys are more likely to be taken on these outings. To what extent are boys/young men benefiting more from the funding than are girls/young women?

Not all alternative approaches are based on one-off activities. A wide range of medium to long-term alternative activities with a youth diversion focus is in place right around the country. Programmes and activities like those outlined above undoubtedly impact positively on the quality of life of the participants. However, the degree to which this is achieved is in direct relation to the quality of the programme itself, which in turn is affected by the level of finance, the quality of the staffing, the degree of consultation and participation in decision-making by the participants. In terms of the actual impact of these programmes on alcohol/drug consumption, it would appear that it is not hugely significant. Klitzner (1987), quoted in Kiely and Egan (2000, p. 47), concludes that:

> While programmes may lead to improved self-esteem and better community involvement or "belongingness" initiatives based on an alternative approach are ineffective alone, in relation to drug use prevention.

The Young People's Facilities and Services Fund (YPFSF) funds many of these activities. This source of funding has enabled many community groups and statutory bodies to provide stimulating and enjoyable activities for groups of young people marginalised by poverty and other forms of disadvantage. Given the government's ongoing commitment to support the YPFSF, the perceived gains must outweigh the costs.

Outreach Worker Approach

According to Riley and O'Hare (2000, p. 129), the task of outreach workers is fourfold:

- Reaching the unreachable
- Assisting the survivors
- Extending service utilisation
- Using an early warning system.

Rhodes and Stimson (1998, p. 155) distinguish between professionally employed workers and locally based outreach workers. Outreach work is an integral part of the drug services provided by the Eastern Health Board. It aims at one-to-one contact with drug users who are not in touch with treatment services and offers advice to untreated drug users and also provides health care by referring users to treatment agencies; the users are then free to access them or not.

Barker (1998, p. 63) raises a number of concerns about the ability of outreach workers and those involved in promoting alternative activities to meet the real needs of drug users. Primarily, she is concerned about the level of training and the level of skills that outreach workers have. The area is dominated by what she calls paraprofessionals who have received little formal training. What, she wonders, is their understanding of what she calls "psychopharmacology and the pathology of addiction"?

Barker's mindset may very well be the result of a credentialist mindset that views workers in a field as unqualified unless they have been through certified courses and does not allow sufficiently for experienced-based learning and the value of knowing one's community. Most outreach workers do not claim to be specialists and are quite prepared to refer people on, as in the case with the Eastern Health Board outreach workers, to other professionals with specific specialisms.

Locally based outreach workers have the advantage of knowing the area and the people in a way that professional workers can never know. They are in a much better position to participate in particular initiatives like peer education programmes, as outlined above.

By building up a solid network of street contacts, and presuming the outreach worker is well regarded, contact should ensue with at least some of the vulnerable, marginalised and hard-to-reach groups like prostitutes, homeless people and drug addicts. What happens as a result of the contact will depend on a number of variables, the most important of which is the predisposition of the target group.

Public Information Campaigns

Governments, or agencies acting on their behalf, generally initiate public campaigns. They have high visibility. Public campaigns usually take the form of billboard postering, TV and radio advertising and newsprint advertising. The campaigns themselves are usually designed by professional media consultants, people very often far removed from the problematised drug use. Such campaigns rely on getting a simple message across and, given the complex nature of the drug issue, simplifying the issue is not always the most appropriate strategy.

Campaign slogans tend to adopt an attitude of "one size fits all situations", so they generally are not sensitive to local, social, cultural or economic factors. Not only that, the possibility of people interpreting the message in a way that was never intended is quite high. Two such campaigns were launched in Britain in the early 1990s. *Heroin Screws You Up* and *Don't Die of Ignorance* were the two slogans used. The "heroin screws you up" campaign featured a poster of a waif-like young person, intending that such an image would discourage drug consumption. The advertisers did not realise that the image used on the poster was similar to ones used by Calvin Klein and was a sought-after image by many fashion-conscious young people. For some, mainly women, suffering from anorexia nervosa or other eating disorders, the image was in fact no disincentive.

Reflecting on the campaign, Plant and Plant (1992, p. 135) argue that human behaviour is influenced by a host of powerful factors and preventing or even minimising health risks is an ambitious objective. Such images do not lead to behaviour change. Agreeing, Bloor and Wood (1998, p. 92) argue that the campaign ran counter to "received research which concluded that such campaigns should not be attempted and were potentially counter productive".

As a result of the First Task Force on Drugs (1996), an Irish poster campaign was launched with the message *Drugs destroy lives, not just of users but people close to them.* Submissions received by the Second Task Force Report expressed the view that the campaign, which concentrated on delivering a "NO" message, was not properly focused and more emphasis should have been put on harm reduction. Commenting on these submissions, the Second Task Force noted that "a highly educated and sophisticated younger population are not satisfied with a simple 'NO' message" (1997, p. 45). The Report goes on to say that "the evidence received by us would appear to support the view that a significant number of young people do not believe that all drugs are dangerous" (1997, p. 45). The Taoiseach in his address at the launch of the National Drugs Strategy 2001-2008 recognised the limitations of a "Just Say No" campaign. This approach, the Taoiseach said, "ignored all sorts of basic issues fundamental to reducing drug misuse" (2001).

Managing Risk

People in their teenage years are at their physical peak and often view themselves as invulnerable and are not conscious of their own vulnerability. This is also the age in which young people are most likely to be risk-loving rather than risk-averse. Plant and Plant (1992, p. 115) are of the view that risk-taking and experimentation during adolescence is normal behaviour as it enables adolescents achieve "independence, identity and maturity".

But risk-taking is also associated with mortality. Road traffic data, for example, highlights the devastating impact of high-risk behaviour. In 1995, 3,019 men and 193 women were prosecuted for driving or attempting to drive a car while drunk or with a blood/urine/alcohol concentration above the prescribed limit (Garda Síochána Annual Report, 1996). The following year, 31 male and 3 female drivers aged between 15 and 24 were killed on Irish roads. Dangerous driving and high-risk behaviour on the roads reflects an unfounded belief in immunity from danger and death not only for oneself but also for others with whom the risk-takers come into contact.

Another type of risk behaviour results in adolescent pregnancy. Many young people engage in unprotected or high-risk sex believing in their personal immunity from an unplanned pregnancy or sexually transmitted diseases. Similarly, many young people who engage in risky drug use perceive themselves to be immune from its worst excesses.

Apart from the damage many drugs may do to the health of drug users, injecting is the highest risk method of injecting drugs. Injecting is strongly related to the spread of infectious diseases like HIV, hepatitis B and C, as well as being strongly related to the spread of fatal and non-fatal drug overdoses.

The degree to which people of all ages expose themselves to and manage risk can determine their life chances. The ability of young people to manage risk is one the keys that will enable them to pass safely from adolescence to adulthood and is also one of the keys to drug education. The Junior Cycle Social, Personal and Health (SPHE) programme includes a small section on Personal Safety (Department of Education and Science, 2000, p. 26). The Department's *Exploring Masculinities* programme also promotes the concept of personal safety.

However, risk and risk management should not be presented as just a response to individual foibles and frailties or individual capriciousness and waywardness. There is a strong correlation between risk and deprivation. The poor are more exposed to risk than are the well-off and have fewer resources at their disposal to counter their vulnerability from risk. The *World Development Report 2000/2001* differentiates between three different types of risk. Micro risks refer to the convulsions or shocks that affect individuals or families. Meso risks affect groups of households or an entire community or village. Macro risks threaten whole societies and countries. However, within households and communities, all the members of the household or community do not always equally share the risk. The *Report* highlights the iniquitous way in which risk affects the household. Studies of vulnerable households indicate that women suffer disproportionately from the shocks and strains when they hit. Children too are often the first to suffer in times of crisis but even here the effects are not always the same — boys in some instances and in some cultures are more cushioned than are girls from the worst effects of strain. There is, for example, a reportedly pro-male bias in some nutritional and restorative responses to shocks like famine and drought.

Debilitating and addictive drug use and related health issues like the prevalence of HIV/AIDS and Hepatitis B and C pose micro, meso and macro risks but the ability to even begin to withstand these risks is directly related to one's socio-economic strength and resourcefulness. While the vulnerability from risk is multidimensional, it has an economic base.

Responses to risk posed by external factors of whatever origin can be categorised according to the *World Development Report 2000–2001* as *"risk reduction* — reducing the probability of shock; and *coping measures* — actions in response to shock" (World Bank, 2001, p. 141). According to the *Report*, the bulk of risk management is directed at devising and implementing *coping measures* but argues that the more urgent and appropriate response is to develop *risk reduction* measures. Safety nets need to be put in place, according to the *Report*, before adverse shocks hit, therefore at best negating their necessity or at worst reducing the demand for these safety nets. These safety nets require multi-faceted interventions, whether the shock comes from debilitating drug use or from famine, HIV/AIDS or environmental destruction.

Given that young people are subject to certain self- and externally perpetuated risks, some of which have very serious consequences not only for their own lives but also for others, a risk management educational intervention, in conjunction with a decision-making intervention might be an appropriate response to their needs. As with all interventions, if this is to have any meaning, risk management needs to be presented without hyperbole and without attempting to constrain youthful zestfulness.

Theatre and Arts-Based Approaches

A number of theatre and arts-based approaches in a harm reduction context have taken place around Ireland. CAFE (Creative Arts For Everyone) was established in 1983 to promote arts as "a collective and liberating artform that creates a voice for social and cultural equality" (National Social Services Board, 2000, p. 32). When contacted, a CAFE representative said that there have been a number of community-based educational programmes with drugs as a central theme. However, nothing has been written about these initiatives.

Kiely and Egan (2000, p. 91ff) reviewed both the process and the outcome of *The Changeling*, devised by Graffiti Theatre

Company, which has been providing Theatre In Education (TIE) in Munster and South Leinster since 1984. The company has been funded by the Arts Council since 1987 and has achieved national and international recognition for excellence. *The Changeling* and the pre-school sister play *Jackie's Day* were designed to work with "Young people on the development of skills and self-awareness in the context of substance misuse prevention" and with "teachers towards skill development in creative and effective approaches to dealing with issues of substance misuse".

Given the difficulty of establishing cause and effect and that behavioural change cannot for obvious reasons be measured for some time, it is difficult to assess the impact of such an intervention. Beyond stating how parents, teachers and students reacted to the performance (very well apparently), it was difficult for Kiely and Egan (2000) to commit themselves further.

In this country, limited use has been made of music mixing, creative dance and movement training as ways of engaging young people in drug education. Where these have taken place, the focus has been on empowering youth leaders to use dance and movement as a developmental tool for working with young people. As well as exposing disadvantaged young people to a new and expressive art form, which hitherto was viewed as highbrow and beyond their reach, one dance project provided young people with an opportunity to be involved in a high-quality, big-budget production in a local theatre. The project was invited to participate in the Discovery Through Dance exchange programme underlining the opportunities for transnational exchange programmes and other opportunities that can result from integrating one's activities into the broader education/youth/training network. Apart from these spin-off benefits, participation in dance and movement in itself is very much worth pursuing, given the difficulty some young people have of verbally articulating what they feel.

Computer Clubhouse

A computer clubhouse is described as a "specific, innovative use of computers, multimedia and other information and communication technologies to help ensure the personal, social and future economic wellbeing of minors between the ages of 7 and 17" (O'Shea, 1999). Conceived and developed by the Massachusetts Institute of Technology (MIT) for children from deprived areas, it was designed to provide inner-city young people with access to new technologies. While middle-class young people generally have many opportunities to develop in a whole range of areas, the same cannot be said for many of their more socially and economically deprived counterparts. In bringing young people to computers, the aim is to redress the imbalance between the technology haves and have-nots.

As in other areas of education, the computer clubhouse is not just about access; it is equally concerned with issues of participation, about identifying new ways of learning and of engaging young people's interests in this still relatively new technology. The goal is not just to provide a few classes to teach a few skills but to enable participants "express themselves fluently with new technology" (Resnick and Rusk, 1996, p. 2). Resnick and Rusk summarise the work of the computer clubhouse as follows:

> young people become designers and creators — not just consumers — of computer-based products. Participants use leading-edge software to create their own artwork, animations, simulations, multimedia presentations, virtual worlds, musical creations, websites, and robotic constructions.

Young people are free to come and go as they wish. There are no attendance sheets, there are no compulsory times; they can "drop in" whenever the clubhouse is open. Central to the computer clubhouse ethos is respect for the learner by building good working relations between the voluntary mentors who work with them. The young people are given access to very expensive equipment and are encouraged to use it creatively and for their own enjoyment.

The first clubhouse was opened in 1993, and during its first two years of operation it attracted more than a thousand young people between the ages of 10 and 16, with 98 per cent coming from socially deprived communities: African American (61 per cent), Asian (13 per cent), and Latino (11 per cent).

The concept has been taken up in fourteen other states within the United States and four countries outside the US — Colombia, Germany, Israel and the Netherlands.

The Internet

For up-to-the-minute information on everything you need to know about drugs — from references to professional journals to animated films, from preventative strategies/goals to harm reduction strategies/goals — the Internet is without parallel. The availability of such a mass of information is in itself problematic. Unreliability of sources, inaccurate information and the trading of information on manufacture of illegal drugs, particularly synthetic, are but some of the difficulties posed by the Internet. Cognisant of such dangers, the European Parliament and the Council of Ministers adopted a multi-annual community action plan on promoting safer use of the Internet (Decision No. 276/1999/EC). However, responsibility for prosecuting and punishing those responsible for illegal content remains with the national law enforcement agencies.

Two UK-based Internet sites have a particularly strong track record for providing reliable information. Drug Scope is the UK's leading centre of expertise on drugs and acts as the UK reporting agency for the European Monitoring Centre for Drugs and Drug Addiction (EMCDDA). Drug Scope is particularly concerned with the provision of more and better services for young people and for those from different ethnic backgrounds.

Targeting service providers and policy makers, it has the twin aims of informing policy-makers and reducing drug-related risk based on the provision of accurate information. In its media guide for writing about drugs in January 2003, it succinctly and, with reference to the latest research, answers commonly asked questions. Are drugs frequently adulterated? (No.) Does cannabis lead people to use hard drugs? (Rarely.) Of all drugs, does cannabis cause the most brain damage? (No, alcohol does.) It also includes an A–Z on drugs as well as a list of reading and a host of other valuable information.

Founded in 1963, Turning Point has worked with people experiencing drug-related problems, HIV, mental health problems and with learning disabilities. It produces an e-magazine, *Drugsworld*, which, in contrast with the Drug Scope site, is more geared towards the needs of the drug user, with a clear harm reduction perspective. The July 2001 magazine, for example, includes a self-assessment for dance drugs as well as cartoons and a four-minute animated film featuring two cats called Creamy and Meatball and their guide Geronimo the dog.

The Department of Health and Children launched a "cool choices" website to try to dissuade teenagers from drinking alcohol. Young people were completely underwhelmed by it and, according to a report in the *Sunday Tribune* (15 July 2001), it was taken off the Internet. According to the newspaper, the site was branded as "childish, patronising and preachy".

Given the very negative reaction to the site, much work remains to be done in this country both at the level of design and use of the Internet as an educational tool. According to the National Centre for Technology in Education, the level of use of the Internet in the formal second-level educational system is low. Access in schools is very limited. Only 20 per cent have ISDN lines and while all other schools have five hours free access, line limitation seriously restricts use.

Dance Safety

Given the importance that dance clubs played in initially bringing illicit drugs, particularly ecstasy, to people and given that this pattern has continued unabated for the past two decades, it is not surprising that those concerned with the welfare of clubbers should seek ways to minimise the risks involved. Given that dance safety is an unambiguous harm reduction strategy, it rests very much on that end of the harm reduction-prevention continuum. Dance safety, according to the guidelines issued by the London Safety Dance campaign, targets not only the clubbers but also the club owners. Advice to the clubbers includes (London Drug Policy Forum, 1996, pp. 5–12):

• Not to buy from strangers or in the dark

• Limit the amount of money they intend spending

• Avoid mixing drugs or injecting alone

- Wear loose cool clothing for dancing

- Eat before going to the club as food provides energy for dancing and lines the stomach.

Advice to the club owners includes:

- Provide free unrestrained access to cold drinking water

- Have adequate ventilation

- Have a relaxed dress code so that patrons can remove clothing without upsetting the management

- Provide a chill-out room.

The publication of these guidelines is, according to the London Drug Policy Forum, a result of "the sheer scale of illicit drug use and the extent to which it has become enmeshed in dance and youth culture" (London Drug Policy Forum, 1996, p. 3). The majority of deaths in clubs according to the Forum have resulted from acute hypothermia or heat stroke and these could have easily been avoided. The focus of the Forum in publishing its guidelines was not just to minimise risk but also to ensure greater and safer enjoyment.

HOUSING LEGISLATION AND ANTI-SOCIAL BEHAVIOUR INTERVENTIONS

This intervention and the two that follow are not educational interventions but are included here because of their popularity with the public and because each has in its own way attracted public comment.

Housing legislation has been enacted recently as a supply-side measure to counter anti-social behaviour and drug-dealing within public sector housing estates. Section 62 of the 1966 Housing Act enables local authorities to recover possession of a dwelling under certain circumstances. No evidence is required of the landlord (i.e. the relevant local authority) but the Act demands that fair procedures are applied.

The Housing (Miscellaneous Provisions) Act came into force in July 1997. The Bill was enacted as a result of the high level of

drug use and the impact of such usage on the lives of many local authority residents. The Act included the Exclusion Order
intended to respond to drug-dealing, harassment and violence.
Anti-social behaviour is defined in the Act as follows:

> the manufacture, production, preparation, importation, ex-
> portation, sale, supply, possession for the purpose of sale or
> supply, or distribution of a controlled drug (within the
> meaning of the Misuse of Drugs Acts 1997).

> (b) any behaviour which causes or is likely to cause any
> significant or persistent danger, injury, damage, loss or fear
> to any person living, working or otherwise lawfully in or in
> the vicinity of a house provided by a housing authority un-
> der the Housing Acts, 1966 to 1977, or a housing estate in
> which the house is situated and without prejudice to the
> foregoing, includes violence, threats, intimidation, coer-
> cion, harassment or serious obstruction of any person.

The Housing Authority must ensure that it is easy to make a
complaint and that would-be complainants are not deterred. In
response to the legislation, various councils/corporations have
clearly established policies with regard to anti-social behaviour. Some have established dedicated anti-social behaviour
units. South Dublin County Council has such a unit and its policy
is to evict any family member that is guilty of serious anti-social
behaviour. The Council receives about 1,000 complaints annually and by 2001 approximately 60 dwellings have been repos-
sessed, three of which only required a court order. The Council
has set up two Anti-Social Response Units with two staff members each. The Council has a three-pronged approach to tackling issues of anti-social behaviour:

- In-fill housing with a view to eliminating open spaces where
  anti-social behaviour is concentrated

- Estate improvement programmes involving laneway closure, more lighting, traffic calming

- Refurbishment programme (COCAD, 1999, p. 15).

Dun Laoghaire/Rathdown County Council, which also has an anti-social behaviour unit, will refuse a house to an applicant who has been found guilty of anti-social behaviour. A staff member of the Council describes the procedures as follows:

- The anti-social inspector/team investigates complaints.

- Complaints cannot be anonymous.

- Complaints will be confidential.

- Any formal complaint will be investigated, the party being complained of will either be invited to the County Council offices or an investigating officer will go out and meet with them in their home.

- If substantiated, a warning letter will be sent stating that the County Council will soon proceed with a notice to quit.

- The tenant will be monitored for change/reform.

- If the tenant does not alter the offending practices, a Notice to quit is issued.

- A court hearing takes place at Circuit Court level.

- If the court hearing is successful, the tenant is legally evicted (COCAD, 1999, p. 14).

In 1998, Dublin Corporation evicted 45 tenants, 30 in 1999, 14 in 2000, 12 in 2001 and 8 in 2002. The significant reduction in the numbers of those being evicted is a result of the seriousness with which the Corporation, now Dublin City Council, is seen to act in relation to anti-social behaviour, according to one spokesperson of the Council.

In the Dublin Corporation Tenants' Handbook and the Tenants' Charter for Ballymun, there is a clear statement that if someone engages in anti-social behaviour and are evicted as a consequence of their actions, they are deemed to have made themselves homeless. According to Declan Wallace of Dublin Corporation:

> Dublin Corporation feels it has broken the back of drug dealing in estates and complexes and it is now time to look

at innovative approaches to dealing with drug users who
live in communities. (COCAD, 1999, p. 17)

The fight against anti-social behaviour is one whose success is
dependent primarily on the ability of people to work together
and to pool information in a combined effort to create an environment in which such activities become unacceptable. The
evidence from Dublin would suggest that tackling anti-social
behaviour has been given added impetus as a result of the establishment of dedicated anti-social behaviour units.

Adopting this approach, while understandable in its objective to improve the quality of life in urban working-class estates,
is hugely problematic. The introduction of the Act attracted
much criticism from civil liberty and human rights activists.

Denying someone access to their home could be regarded
as a serious infringement of their human rights unless it can be
established beyond reasonable doubt that they pose a serious
threat either to their own family or to the local community. Even
in those circumstances and where a criminal act has not been
recorded, there would appear to be grounds for concern.
There are also serious implications for others members of the
family who may be forced to move too — members of the family
who may have been neither involved nor supported dealing
with drugs. It also poses questions as to where these people go
and what society's broader obligation to them is. The exclusion
of people from public sector housing for anti-social behaviour
was thrown into sharp relief in early 2003 when one man who
had been excluded died while sleeping in front of his boarded-
up house. His death challenges the policy and practice of exclusion and re-focuses attention on the rights of the excluded.

Furthermore, if they are to be resettled, what rights do
families have in the area where the family/individual is being
relocated? Should they have any? While recognising the destructive and pernicious influence that anti-social behaviour can
have in any community, should such behaviour be dealt with
through due process in the criminal courts, rather than through
the housing authority? The Act only applies to residents of public sector housing, thereby disproportionately affecting poor
families. Expecting a local authority to act as evictor runs

counter to its role as housing agent and instead of dealing with housing shortages and homelessness, the authority runs the risk of causing homelessness.

TACKLING DRUG DEALING THROUGH COMMUNITY POLICING

An article in *Poverty Today* concluded that "It is generally agreed that community–Garda relationships have not been good in many, if not all, of those areas worst hit by the drugs crisis" (Supply Control Committee of the Inter-Agency Drugs Project [North Inner City Dublin], 1998, p. 13).

The Inter-Agency Drugs Project (IADP) was established in October 1995 with funding from the Departments of Justice, Health, Education and Social Welfare, recognising a need for change in policing strategies. Negotiations around a community policing structure, which would have various levels of account-ability, resulted in the proposed Community Policing and Es-tate Management Forum (CPEMF). The objectives of the Forum were to:

- Ensure that the law is effectively enforced against those in-volved in the supply and trafficking of illegal drugs, espe-cially heroin;

- Reduce the amount of drug-related crime and social nui-sance;

- Co-ordinate a common community Garda strategy against drug dealing;

- Improve community–Garda relations and communications and provide a clear conduit for information exchange;

- Develop a formal structure for community–Garda concilia-tion;

- Have formal consultations with residents' and tenants' groups, promote estate developments and improve estate supervision, including dealing with anti-social behaviour, problem tenants and squatters (CityWide, 1998).

The Rialto Policing Forum is one such forum. It consists of four public representatives, three Gardaí, twelve to fourteen residents, six community workers, one official from Dublin Corporation, one school principal and an independent chairperson. It drafted the following mission statement:

> An ongoing planned and shared operation in the area whereby issues of mistrust and suspicion can be explored by means of mediation. Information and feedback will be enabled in a structured way. Research and evaluation will be carried out to ascertain the most effective model of community policing. A continual proactive and sustained Garda presence is guaranteed . . . (CityWide, 1998).

Mistrust of police forces is not unique to Ireland. Given that the use of illicit drugs automatically puts one outside the law, the possibility of a collision with those obligated to uphold the law is ever present. Distrust of law enforcers is not just confined to those who consume drugs. Despite society's general reliance on police forces, there remains, particularly amongst those marginalised from the state, an air of suspicion about one of the most visible manifestations of the state. In some cases, that suspicion and distrust is reciprocated. Hence, there is a very real need for community policing structures that are not just perceived as talking shops but have some serious contribution to ensuring that individuals and communities feel secure.

SURVEILLANCE AND ZERO TOLERANCE APPROACH

In stark contrast to much of the above, there still exists a strong constituency that argues for zero tolerance of drug use and advocates a strong deterrent approach. Former Justice, Equality and Law Reform Minister John O'Donoghue is regarded as the Irish architect of zero tolerance. Speaking in the Seanad during the debate (1997) on the Criminal Justice No. 2 Bill, the Minister strongly defended zero tolerance. The main provision of the Bill was the introduction of mandatory sentencing for drug trafficking to the value of £10,000 or more. The bill also proposed detaining persons suspected of drug trafficking for up to seven days. In introducing the Bill, the Minister said:

the fact that this major criminal law reform measure is being introduced so early in the lifetime of this government is clear practical evidence of the government's policy of zero tolerance towards crime. (O'Donoghue, 1997)

As well as the introduction of stiffer penalties, there was also greater demand for surveillance of citizens. The traditional caricature of community surveillance from behind the squinting window has been replaced by surveillance by closed-circuit television (CCTV). This involves the placing of video cameras in what are regarded as flashpoints in a neighbourhood or in an inner-city area that will monitor the behaviour of passers-by. The Brave New World of technology has changed surveillance from the local to the bureaucratic in what Carlen and Morgan (1999, p. 76) call "the rise of the stranger society".

Reviewing the operations of such systems, Carlen and Morgan (1999, p. 89) observe that in situations where cameras are manually controlled, "the gaze of the camera does not fall equally on all users of the street". In the US, there is a massive overrepresentation of young black men in shot while other factors that catch the camera's eye include dress and deportment.

Zero tolerance, which was debated at some length in this country during the 1997 general election, is given short shift by Dorn and Lee (1999, p. 90) as a suitable response to drug users. They regard it as "narrow, uncompromising and aggressive and by its very nature targets people rather than underlying problems". Like CCTV, the targets are low-income, public-sector dwellers, males, and people from minority ethnic groups. Neither approach has any credibility with people working with users or with the users themselves.

Emphatically rejecting such approaches, Carlen and Morgan (1999, p. 163) conclude that young people have received "more control than care, more blame than apology and have more restrictions placed upon them than rights, positive status and personal freedoms bestowed".

CONCLUSION

This chapter has outlined fourteen different types of interventions. What is clear from the above review is that there is no one simple, "one size fits all" solution. Reviewing these and other kinds of initiatives, Flynn (2001) comes to two conclusions. The first is that the severity of legal sanction, zero tolerance or increased surveillance does not appear to have any impact on drug consumption patterns. The second conclusion is that measures designed to promote abstinence are largely a waste of taxpayers' money.

With regard to the quality of school-based educational interventions that have been outlined above, Morgan (2001) urges caution. Not surprisingly, those involved in various projects tend to "talk up" their work and its effectiveness. Saying this does not in any way disparage the work that is happening, often in very difficult circumstances. In many cases, motivation of workers requires that they adopt the pint-half-full rather than the pint-half-empty option. In contrast, those who come from the outside tend to take a less sanguine view of the intervention. In particular, external evaluators/researchers have "been sharply critical of the way in which data from school-based prevention evaluations have been presented and, in some cases, have suggested that there has been a tendency to exaggerate positive outcomes while ignoring negative ones" (Morgan, 2001, p. 36). This is partly to do with expectation. Modest interventions should carry with them modest expectations.

When it comes to deciding what is an appropriate intervention, there will always be preferred options or preferred series of options, depending on one's ideological perspective and the nature of the target group, among other factors. However, most people connected with the range of issues associated with drug use agree with the Taoiseach's assessment when he stated in launching the National Drugs Strategy 2001–2008 that "tackling the issue requires both a multidimensional approach and an integrated series of short, medium and long-term actions". These actions, if they are to have any meaning, must be undertaken in the context of radical social and economic investment in deprived communities and must be underpinned by a strong respect for human rights.

Chapter 5

Summary: The Politics of Drugs

Close scrutiny of current drug policy in this country indicates a divided and occasionally conflicting policy paradigm. While the rhetoric is impressive, the willingness to match that with real investment appears to be sadly lacking. Given the changed circumstances of the Irish economy in 2002/3, the fear is that the best opportunity we had in the history of this state to effect egalitarian policies has been squandered.

Close scrutiny of international policies indicates an equally divided paradigm. With the exception of Britain, there is an increasing gulf opening up between western European countries and the US response to the dramatic growth in drugs consumption. This is manifested not only in the growing divergence on the justification for a militarised war on drugs but also in the growing divergence on the justification for a war on terrorism.

As stated in Chapter One, much of the debate on drugs that has taken place has been characterised by closure and shallowness rather than by openness and depth. Dualism has characterised the debate. Those "who ply their evil trade", inhabit one end of a continuum and are counterbalanced by those who see intoxication as a human right and a liberation from life's daily grind. What is clear is that people continue to differ about the way in which all drugs continue to affect society and the escalation of drug use continues to confront society with serious dilemmas.

Irrespective of ideological background, all are agreed that drug use has escalated enormously in the last four decades, and that the use of mood-altering and mind-changing drugs is not just a recent phenomenon. Various cultures dating back to antiquity in different parts of the world have, with little or no sanction, used an array of substances to induce good feelings as well as to distract themselves from the harsh realities of daily living. Opium dates back at least to the Ancient Greeks and references to marijuana appear in early Persian, Hindu, Greek, Arab and Chinese writings. The chewing of coca in the Inca Empire was practised for centuries.

 In this century, in what is perceived as a glaring inconsistency by many people, substances like alcohol and cigarettes that temporarily induce good feelings are sanctioned as acceptable. For a substantial number of individuals and their families, their consumption exacts a heavy price. Yet other substances, that many would claim are less harmful, are strongly prohibited and their use criminalised. Not only that, it would appear that the consumption of banned substances is perceived as more problematic if consumed by certain sections of the population.

Young people, particularly young men, working class people, nomadic people, Black, Hispanic, African American and Asian people's drug consumption is subject to higher levels of surveillance and condemnation. Consumption patterns do not always reflect the level of disapprobation or the same punitive response. University students, mainstream middle classes and older people, it would appear, are exempt from the moral opprobrium that is reserved for the less advantaged.

Since the start of the twentieth century, particular kinds of drugs have been problematised and criminalised while other kinds of drugs have been sanctioned in what would appear to have been a very arbitrary process. The sanctioning of some drugs has resulted in enormous profits for some, while the criminalisation of other drugs has resulted in enormous destruction and loss. Much of this loss and destruction has accrued from the war on drugs.

In a seemingly seamless continuity of policy, each president of the United States since the Second World War has identified a particular war that characterises his presidency. In some cases, the war baton is passed from one president to the next. The war on drugs is one such war. Nixon's war on drugs became Reagan's, Bush's and Clinton's and the younger Bush's war on drugs and this war became linked into a broader war on terrorism. The ferocity and tenacity with which this war has been fought by each successive president increased by the decade. The cost of the war is taking a heavy toll on the people of the South and the Southeast, their environment, economy, traditions and cultures. Ultimately, it is also costing some people of the United States, particularly the poor and the middle classes. The funding that might in other circumstances be spent on social, educational and health programmes is instead spent on weapons and armaments.

Three countries in South America have paid an inordinately heavy price and of these Colombia has and is paying the heaviest. There the war on drugs is commingled with the war on terrorism resulting in the death of tens of thousands of people. As in the other wars in which the US is involved, public consciousness becomes fixated with one or possibly two figures that are constructed as the epitome of evil. Osama bin Laden and Saddam Hussein personify the ogre that threatens American interests in the early part of the twenty-first century while the Colombian drug magnate Pablo Escobar fulfilled that role for a number of years in Colombia. His execution was relentlessly pursued by the United States without regard to the death toll or without due concern with the actions of their collaborators, many of whom were themselves actively involved in drug trafficking.

Ostensibly, US policy objective is to cut drug supply thereby reducing the demand and addressing the many social problems that can ensue from the consumption of drugs. In the world of *realpolitik*, its policy is very different. In Vietnam, Cambodia, Laos, Central and South America and Afghanistan, US intelligence agencies have colluded in and actively supported those whom it temporarily considers useful in the furtherance of their strategic aims of overall global domination. From Vang Pao in Laos, through to Oliver North's funding schemes for the Contra war against the democratically elected government of Daniel Ortega in Nicaragua, and culminating with the collaboration with the Northern Alliance in Afghanistan, the US has never balked at collaborating with drug traffickers. These collaborations occur while officially pursuing a virulently anti-illicit drug campaign.

Where the US goes Britain follows in the international geopolitical power struggle. Its instincts are to follow Washington rather than Brussels. Britain part-justified its involvement in the war in Afghanistan on the basis that it was fighting the war on drugs and that it was protecting British youth. European policy in general has adopted a less punitive approach than either Britain or the United States. Switzerland and the Netherlands in particular have been to the fore in promoting harm reduction strategies/goals that recognise that drug consumption is and will continue to be a feature of contemporary life as it has in life in the past. Recognising that the expectation that people will buy into abstinence are unrealistic, they have sought to put in place a series of measures that will reduce the harm that addictive drug use can cause. In an unexpected break with previous policy in 2002, Britain formally stepped on to the decriminalisation path.

Irish policy lives somewhere between the two. Rattled by the death of journalist Veronica Guerin, the government introduced a raft of legislation to counter drug trafficking. It also continues to adopt a punitive approach to drug use. Side by side with this approach, the government recognises that community engagement is important in addressing problems associated with drug use and to this extent has put in place a regional structure involving community groups to devise ways of responding to local drug-related difficulties.

In Ireland, as elsewhere, not all drug use is problematised and not all drugs are problematised. Without doubt, serious and persistent drug use that debilitates and dominates all human interaction is problematic, not just for those directly affected but also for their families, communities and for the broader society. Serious, chronic drug-taking is linked to, though not necessarily exclusively dependent on, high levels of social alienation and material deprivation. Structural inequalities are the single biggest contributor to drug use while acknowledging that not everyone in a disadvantaged community will use drugs or, conversely, that people in advantaged communities will not use drugs or become dependent on them.

Recreational, non-dependent drug use generally gets very little attention, as it does not conform to the addiction and problematised paradigm. However, feeding recreational use inevitably contributes to the blurring of the distinction between what is legal and illegal. Certainly, there is a growing tolerance of recreational drug use, but no clear consensus exists as to what the consequences are to this low, occasional level of use or what should be the most appropriate policy response. While some countries have either tacitly or explicitly allowed the sale and possession of small amounts for personal use, others are deeply distrustful of what they regard as the creeping acceptance of drugs.

The way in which users are perceived varies hugely. What is important in this debate is that users are seen first and foremost as people, perhaps people with difficulties, perhaps predisposed to addiction, perhaps not afforded the same life opportunities that others were, perhaps difficult people with whom to engage, but people nevertheless. How one views the person who uses and abuses addictive substances, legal or illegal, will determine how one responds to them. In this context, it is worth remembering the response of Gerry Raftery OFM of Merchant's Quay Ireland that the only response is to assert "the innate dignity of each person no matter how terrible their circumstances" (Merchant's Quay Project, 1999, p. 2).

Clearly that is not the case now nor has it been since the first moves were instigated to criminalise the use of some drugs. Initial demands for criminalisation of drugs were clearly racially tinged. Fear of difference, fear of contamination, fear of chocolatisation (the browning of the population) underpinned the more strident calls for criminalisation. The accusation was made that drugs were undermining White racial purity and Black men and men of other racial groups were targeted in particular as a threat to White integrity. Thus, drugs scare tactics became part of the creation of a *them and us* mentality. Black and Chinese people soon became the feared *other*, the *foreigner* in our (White) midst. Controlling drugs was one way of controlling the perceived excess of these people from racial minorities. While governments are happy to locate the "problem" of drug consumption on outside forces, there is a growing recognition that the "problem" is demand- as much as supply-led. More and more work has been done to reduce or to better manage the demand. There is general recognition that there is no one solution for how countries ought to respond. There are no templates. Harm reduction is one broad approach that has attracted attention but the details of how it actually operates in practice remain unclear. However, harm reduction is seen by many as conceding defeat, as giving in, and in doing this acknowledging that the godfathers of this illegal and illicit trade have won the war. For many, that is just a step too far. The proponents of harm reduction, however, argue that in the real world, one has to face up to the reality that drugs are here to stay. The harm they do should be minimised as much as possible and that those who intend experimenting should do so in the knowledge of the facts — facts that should be communicated to them in an accurate dispassionate non-scaremongering way.

To recognise that at least some drug use appears to be recreational does not in any way disavow that for many the harsh reality of their drug use has enslaved their mind and body and in some cases ultimately destroyed them. Some illicit drugs have the capacity to scar not only individuals but also whole communities, leaving bereft families, children without parents and parents without children. Dealing or consuming illicit drugs inevitably brings one into contact with crime and with the nefarious world of ruthless criminals and this reality is unlikely to be changed in the mid- to long-term.

But that is not the whole story: real understanding requires that people go beyond the addiction and criminal paradigms. Great swathes of the world's populations use legal and illegal drugs without ever wrecking social, community and family life, or indeed without adversely impacting on their own life expectancy. Equally, great swathes of the world's population are linked with criminal practices in the so-called developing world. The capitalist economy within which we all live in the western world exploits for our benefit many of the children, their parents, and communities of the South. Whatever one's ideological position or whatever our attitude to drug use, that reality needs to be acknowledged.

Acknowledging that reality does not imply that a *laissez-faire* response be adapted to the increasing use of drugs. Irrespective of the dilemmas they throw up, interventions are needed at a range of levels; interventions that will inform, educate, prevent, reduce harm, treat and rehabilitate, if that is what people want. If such interventions are to be effective they need to be based on informed opinion rather than knee-jerk reactions and political grandstanding. In addressing the issue at local or national level, it is clear that one agency or one intervention acting on its own cannot meaningfully impact on illegal and illicit drug use and this view has been recognised for a long time. Nor can drug issues be addressed in isolation. Inevitably, engaging in drug work brings one into contact with race, ethnicity, gender, sexuality, cultural, human rights and political debates.

The global dimension is central to understanding this whole area. There has been much scapegoating of producing countries and their peoples. Interventionist policies and actions by neo-colonial countries have been undertaken in the guise of, as Tony Blair has said, "choking off" the supply while many are suspicious that other geo-political considerations are at play. The desire for power and control, for global dominance would appear to outweigh the desire to reduce the harm to people. These are not remote considerations for Irish people, many of whom have a strong commitment to the development of fair, just and humane policies in the so-called "developing" but wholly un(der)developed worlds of the South and South East.

The multifaceted approach that is required to enable these countries develop alternative economies need to be replicated closer to home if those currently trading/using drugs are to find alternative ways of living and livelihoods. Redress is needed to undermine years and decades of structural, social and economic inequities. Redress is also required in the areas of the physical environment, education, training, health, housing, employment and recreation. There is now widespread acceptance that approaches need to be multi-component, comprehensive and broad-based and that those who operate on narrow conceptual frameworks will invariably fail. The will and capacity to implement and resource these structural changes does not match the level of rhetoric in which politicians are happy to engage.

In the meantime, there is an urgent need to recognise that illegal drugs are part of the streetscape and the landscape and will be for the foreseeable future. While interventions can be put in place that can contribute to mitigating the worst impact of serious, debilitating and life-threatening drug use, recreational and large-scale and persistent drug use are more than likely here to stay, for the foreseeable future.

This account posed a number of questions at the outset in Chapter One. In the light of the above, these questions are now revisited. In revisiting them, Ross Coomber's admonition that much of the debate on drugs that has taken place has been characterised by closure rather than openness will be kept to the fore.

POLITICS AND THE WAR ON DRUGS

Seismic changes have taken place in international relationships as a result of the atrocities that unfolded in the United States on 11 September 2001. In the aftermath of the assault on the World Trade Centre and the Pentagon and the air crash in Pennsylvania, world attention has focused exclusively on East–West relations. In the meantime, problems in North–South and North–South-East relations continue unabated. The issue of drugs is central to North–South relations, particularly relations with the South American countries of Colombia, Bolivia and Peru.

In the current atmosphere (early 2003), it is difficult to find intellectual and emotional space for the peasant farmers and rural dwellers of these countries and their manifold difficulties. But their difficulties are real and deep-rooted. Equally, their fate and very livelihoods are at the mercy (if not in the same dramatic scale) of decisions taken by western governments, as are the Afghani refugees massed on the Pakistani borders. In 2000, an estimated 35,000 people were killed in Colombia and the numbers whose livelihoods were directly affected is inestimable, many caught in the western-inspired war on drugs. Within Colombia, the war on drugs was undertaken in parallel with the war on terrorism. The concentration of the war in the southern region of the country, the stronghold of the guerrilla organisation FARC, is no mere coincidence. FARC is anathema to the US government because of their perceived Marxist leanings and the United States government is desperately anxious to secure a more compliant administration in Colombia.

Securing compliant administrations not only within what the United States regards as it own geographical backyard or sphere of influence is one of the major foreign policy objectives of successive governments since the Second World War. In its war against Afghanistan, one of its most willing coalition members, Britain linked this component of the war on terrorism with the war on drugs. Both powers have succeeded in establishing a docile subservient administration in Afghanistan. That this new administration is unable to reduce the supply of opium to the same extent as the previous administration did is conveniently overlooked. The main objective of the war was the establishment of an acquiescent government and that objective has been achieved.

War, as a policy response, is a blunt and bloody instrument. The only beneficiaries are the arms manufacturers and their shareholders. The relationship between those who declare war and those who benefit from the economics of war has become worryingly close. The profits from the armaments industry have added erroneously to the wealth of the wealthy. Those who plan and benefit from war never experience war in all its awful gory detail. The war on drugs has been an unmitigated disaster for producers and consumers and has not made any significant impact on supply or demand. It is time to stop this senseless war.

Ireland's commitment to developing countries has been well documented. In recent times, Ireland's track record in supporting, for example, the people of East Timor during the genocide of 1999 was second to none. Two former Foreign Affairs ministers, Dick Spring and David Andrews stood firmly with the people of East Timor, challenging the propaganda of the Indonesian military. Similarly, Irish parliamentary delegates have visited Iraq and along with a number of non-governmental organisations have called for the lifting of the sanctions that are causing untold misery to countless numbers of Iraqi people.

The misery caused by the war on drugs needs to be highlighted in a way that the misery of the people of Iraq and East Timor was highlighted. As well as looking inward, national drug policy needs to consider if it should look outwards and engage in discussions at various global forums on the factors that drive production, particularly heroin and cocaine. In formulating outward-looking policies, consideration should be given to the underlying causes of drug production. Interventions that are primarily focused on the domestic electoral considerations of colonial powers rather than on the needs of indigenous people need to be challenged. To put it another way, government policy needs to articulate a clear policy that the war on drugs has failed and should end. Not only that, but it should also challenge the near-exclusive focus on production of drugs to the neglect of all the intermediary stages through which illicit drugs pass before they reach the consumer in the western world. The almost exclusive preoccupation with the production of drugs in countries of the South and the Southeast also fails to take account of the quantity of synthetic drugs that are produced in the western world for western world production. Instead of allowing the punitive and warlike approach to dominate, human rights need to be brought more to the fore.

Through membership of the United Nations and the European Union, the government ought to challenge the war on drugs in general and *Plan Colombia* and general US policy in South America in particular. Instead of conjuring images of nefarious foreign drug dealers intent on making vast fortunes out of western misery, Irish policy would be better served by highlighting western governments' culpability, through domestic policies that ignore the needs of their most disadvantages citizens to the advantage of the middle and upper classes, in producing the almost insatiable demand for illicit drugs.

DIFFERENCE

It is easy to whip up moral panic. This is particularly so at a time when public media-led discourse takes place in a shrill tone and at high volume, as is currently the case. In this heightened atmosphere it is relatively easy to suggest cause-and-effect relationships and to convince a scarred public that the cause of their fear can be easily identified, that a bogey man exists somewhere in their midst. The foundations on which moral panic is built are very often shaky and transient. Moral panic can be easily created by presenting news and information in a particular way through repeated and selective repetition of certain phenomenon. Certainly moral panic about drugs sells and has an instant appeal to more lurid tabloid journalism. It has always been thus.

In the early part of the last century, minority ethnic groups fulfilled that role of bogeyman in the imaginations of a gullible public manipulated by racist xenophobes. Racism has always had sexual undertones and this can be seen in the way that Blacks, drugs and sex have been triangled. The 1910 Report of the *International Opium Commission*'s claim that cocaine made rapists of Black men and that Blacks achieved immense strength and cunning under its influence is testimony to this triangulation and hence its prohibition.

In different eras, the deaths of Billy Carlton and Len Bias were used to up the moral panic ante and resulted in demands for a crackdown on drugs and drug users. Prior to Carlton's death, newspapers reported that prostitutes were plying soldiers on leave from the front with cocaine in the West End of London with the concomitant risk of undermining the war effort. It was feared that Britain's war effort was going to be undermined by the heady mixture of prostitutes, drugs and Black people.

Neither the moral panic nor the fear of the outsider, *the other*, has abated much since then. This book has alluded to the "moral panic" that existed in response to the dramatically increased level of heroin use in Dublin in the 1980s and which, according to a recent nation-wide survey on drug-related knowledge, attitudes and beliefs, still exists.

Moral panic can be engineered by politicians and pressure groups in their desire not only to gain political advantage over their political opponents, particularly if those opponents are in government, but also to ensure that particular policies can be enacted that might not find favour in more even-keeled times. Those who wish to sell news can also engineer it. Whether the perceived threat is drugs, prostitution, particular racial groups, ethnic minorities, terrorism or a combination of all, civil liberty activists have again and again expressed concern at legislative initiatives implemented in such an atmosphere. In short, moral panic is a poor basis for making laws.

The issue of race and ethnicity has come very much to the fore in Ireland in recent years. Two developments of note have taken place in this country in the last five years: firstly, the increase in the numbers of people newly arrived into this State; and secondly, recent equality legislation protecting the rights of minorities. To what extents both of these developments have impacted on drug-related service provision has yet to be established.

Given that the trend of immigration will more than likely continue in the foreseeable future, now is the time for the National and Local Drugs Task Forces and others working in the field to begin a process of dialogue with asylum seekers and refugees and their service providers and agents. Now is the time to develop an appropriate response that does not stigmatise or feed into racial prejudice. The first of these steps is to question current policy of direct provision to refugees and asylum seekers and their exclusion from the labour market. International experience indicates that exclusion from the formal market results in a flourishing but highly destructive alternative street economy based on the sale of illicit drugs.

Proper and rational debate on the relationship between race and drugs is urgently needed, a debate that does not feature in the National Drugs Strategy 2001–2008. Clearly, politicians, policy-makers and people in positions of power need to be extremely sensitive in the remarks they make to ensure that their comments cannot in any way be seen to feed into xenophobia. This debate must address the issue of consumption by minority racial groups as well as the supply issue. Given that many newly arrived refugees and asylum seekers are housed in inner-city Dublin, and given the level of trauma many have suffered in their home country, inevitably some will come into contact with illegal drugs and with the criminal underworld that supplies these drugs. If specific measures are taken, then we may yet avoid what McGregor sees as Britain's failure to meet the needs of ethnic drug users, a failure that is "a particular blot on British drugs policy" (1998, p. 152).

DILEMMAS

(Re)legalisation

(Re)legalisation is clearly very emotive and there is huge official resistance even to discussion of it as an issue, notwithstanding the call by one hundred members of the European Parliament to legalise cocaine, ecstasy and cannabis and to make heroin available for medicinal purposes. Of all the issues related to drug use, the debate around (re)legalisation is characterised by closure rather than openness to the truths and concerns of the opposing side in this very heavily polarised debate.

Those who resolutely resist any move to change the current status quo argue that dramatically increased use of currently illegal drugs would inevitably ensue in the event of (re)legalisation. The knock-on effect, they argue, in terms of social and community upheaval, not to mention the strain on state services, would be serious and very detrimental. The counter-argument, that (re)legalisation would result in a dramatic decrease in levels of crime by negating the raison d'être of a whole criminal class that currently exists, is dismissed. The wilful, profiteering and murderous environment within which illicit drug-dealing happens in this and other countries would be seriously undermined, the proponents of (re)legalisation argue, if the current policy were to change. Change in current policy would also have the potential to transform the relationships between powers and internationally reduce the need for the current military spend. The very reduction in military spend is in itself a disincentive to (re)legalisation. For many that are opposed to (re)legalisation, the door is firmly closed.

The proponents for change also argue that health-related problems associated with the content and method of ingesting illegal drugs could be addressed if these drugs were (re)legalised. In particular, the current epidemic of HIV/AIDS among intravenous drug-injecting people could be arrested. Such entreaties do not find favour with the prohibitionists.

What current policy-makers are slow to recognise is that we live in that night in which all cats are grey, rather than in continuous broad sunshine that clearly disperses shadowy ambiguous forms. Human nature is complex and convoluted and does not automatically kowtow to legal prohibition. The reality is that we live in an ambiguous world where particular drugs are illegal but tolerated, are publicly condemned but informally condoned, albeit with particular populations and in small measures. The clear blue water that politicians sought to put between licit and illicit drugs is becoming more and more clouded. The boundaries are fraying at the edges and this is becoming more and more the case.

Current policy operates on the "blind eye" principle. It's a fudge, which given the complexity of human nature is not necessarily a bad thing. It could be argued, for example, that the peace process in the North of Ireland was based on fudges to enable participants establish some common ground and experience collective engagement. The dilemma for policymakers is whether or not we as a society are prepared to live with the present fudge, or is it time to confront the reality that current illicit drug consumption is here to stay? Demands for stronger, tougher action on drugs while satisfying certain political constituencies has not in any way led to a reduction in drug use or contributed in any way to addressing the underlying problems that drive production and consumption. Zero tolerance of drug consumption is a blunt instrument and reflects a bureaucratic, centralised and heavy-handed approach to human frailty. It has patently failed as an approach. The criminalisation of drugs from production to consumption has resulted in a catalogue of death, violence, corruption, oppression, anarchy, turmoil and a fatalistic nihilism.

The evidence from this discussion clearly indicates that drugs are not the real problem; rather, they are the presenting symptom or the manifestation of manifold problems. The large-scale consumption of illicit and some licit drugs reflects deeper structural problems. These will never be addressed as long as the focus continues to be on lurid, voyeuristic preoccupation with providers, traffickers, pushers, addicts, with the producers and consumers of illicit drugs. Illicit drug use is not the root of the problem; it is the manifestation of the structural dilemmas that the poor of the world have to confront on a daily basis.

While the debate about (re)legalisation will run and run and while the arguments in its favour are compelling, the prospects for this seismic social change happening in the short to medium term is remote. In the meantime, there is no compelling reason why the structural inequalities that are very much part of the equation cannot begin to be addressed. The (re)legalisation of drugs on its own will not address the lack of basic human rights of the *campesinos* in South America or the peasant farmers in Southeast Asia. Nor on its own will it address the structural disadvantages faced by the residents of East Harlem, inner-city Dublin, Cork and Limerick and elsewhere.

Destructive drug use in these and other places merely reflects their social, cultural, political and economic isolation and powerlessness, a powerlessness that, at least occasionally, breeds vulnerability, anger, self-destructive behaviour, and individual, social and family instability. While there are individual stories and individual variations within each person's story, both producers and socially marginalised addictive users share a common persistent poverty, a poverty that is often located side by side with great wealth and opulence. For those who have access to this wealth and opulence, and who may have become addicted to drugs, they at least have access to every support and service that will enable them, difficult and all as it might be, to come to terms with their addiction. For others, the future is less secure.

(Re)legalising drugs on its own may in fact exacerbate an already difficult situation unless it is matched by a commitment to human rights, education, training, employment, social services provision, family support, an ecologically sustainable environment and a commitment to the provision of a good quality of life for all.

However, there is every possibility that (re)legalisation may actually reduce consumption, particularly in deprived communities, because drugs may become *less* available as street dealing would decline, and if the people living in these areas were presented with real opportunities for personal and social fulfilment, the need for large-scale drug consumption would abate. In short, (re)legalisation, were it ever to happen, would need to be matched with a commitment to redistributive (down) justice. (Re)legalisation would also negate the need for the wildly expensive and, in the case of the United States, privatised incarceration of large numbers of the population.

Those who object to the (re)legalisation of all drugs do so on the basis that it would require massive social engineering on a scale that has not been undertaken heretofore and that such a reorientation carries huge risks. Such claims are, in fact, disingenuous. To suggest that the (re)legalisation of drugs would involve an experiment in social engineering that has not been attempted before is to deny the massive social engineering that is taking place at present. The world economy is currently being re-fashioned by a small elite, representatives of multinational companies, large corporations, financiers, capitalists and so-called captains of technology to their mutual benefit. It is being re-fashioned to the detriment of the poor both in the so-called developed world and in the so-called developing world. This restructuring has been overseen by a compliant political class, many of whom are drawn from the same class or who are politically beholden to these classes as a result of the dependent relationship between corporate funding and political decision-making.

The result of this refashioning is an increase in the democratic deficit, and a turning back of the clock of the social democratic model of public sector interventionism. In the process, the poor, the disabled, many racial and ethnic minorities, many women and the frail have been sidelined and punished for their status. The poor, and many racial and ethnic minorities have been socially and economically ostracised in large numbers in penal institutions or in abandoned neighbourhoods.

A more ethical human rights-based model of social engineering is required. Whether that would involve the (re)legalisation of drugs must remain an open question. It is too soon to effect closure on that debate.

Strategies

(Re)legalisation is not the only dilemma posed by illicit drug consumption. Age, social class, gender, ethnicity, race and sexual orientation are all key variables in attempting to establish a rounded picture of drug use and in trying to challenge the stereotype that drug use is essentially a young male working-class "problem". Each of these variables requires a response. Youth drug use gets significant and, some would argue, disproportionate attention (Chetley, 1995).

The National Drugs Strategy 2001–2008 certainly gives a lot of attention to the young and to their isolation from stable family and communal structures. The Strategy is cognisant of "the complexity of youth culture", seeks to "strengthen resilience amongst young people" and "maximise the effectiveness of school-based programmes" (National Drugs Strategy 2001–2008, p. 98). In focusing on the need for strengthening resilience amongst young people, the Strategy is underscoring individual weaknesses rather than structural inadequacies of the user.

The emphasis is on defective individuals rather than defective communities and societies that tolerate huge social inequities. "Defective individual" theories are deeply flawed, as are cultural theories that deny or downplay the socio-economic injustices that underpin the culture that breeds the bulk of debilitating drug use. Interventions at the individual level will only result in a management approach to consumption, whereas a more fundamental approach that would address employment, education, housing, environment opportunities, choices and rights would have a more fundamental and long-term effect. The individualised, psychological, reductionist blame game has been overplayed.

It is worth repeating Carlen and Morgan's (1999, p. 163) conclusion that "young people have received more control than care, more blame than apology and have more restrictions placed upon them than rights, positive status and personal freedoms bestowed". Perhaps their injunction could be extended to many other sectors of our society, to the consumers as well as the producers of drugs. Individualistic solutions that blame certain sections of society for their foibles and failures fail to recognise the structural transformation that is required.

The Strategy's preoccupation with youth is also evidenced in its declared target to "bring drug misuse by school-goers to below the EU average" (National Drugs Strategy 2001–2008, p. 109). In all, five of the nine key performance indicators relate to the second-level school-going population. No reference is made to the "increase in the use of cocaine, both nationally and internationally among young professionals" (p. 25); or to "the 80 per cent of third level students who were reported in a survey to have taken an illegal drug" (National Drugs Strategy 2001–2008, p. 33).

The general preoccupation with young people is further underlined in the research objectives of the Strategy, of which there are two. One of them relates to "gaining a greater understanding of the factors which contribute to Irish people, particularly young people, misusing drugs" (National Drugs Strategy 2001–2008, p. 111).

The attention to the young may very well result from the dominant perception and the government's desire to be seen to respond to that perception. However, it does raise the question: where do other groups — the young professionals and the third-level student population; the middle-aged and older drug users — fit into national response strategy? The evidence challenges policy-makers to look beyond the young urban male.

Drug use has never just been the preserve of the working classes. Yet there has been disproportionate attention to controlling and prohibiting the consumption habits of the working classes (Walton, 2001), while those who use from the middle and upper classes are left alone to indulge their desire for kicks. The survival instincts of those forced on to the margins and who are confronted with survival on a daily basis with are never given the recognition they deserve. Nor does the defective culturalist perspective hold any water, that those who are caught up in a life of drug abuse are somehow the products of inferior and defective culture. If only they would become more WASPish — sign up to the cultural hegemony of the White Angle-Saxon Protestant ethos that is more and more being used as the defining reference point for acceptable norms and behaviour — then they would not be in such difficulty. Such prejudices need to be challenged.

If working-class males figure strongly in the populist perception of the drug user, so too, according to Khan (2000), Pavee Point (1999) and the EMCDDA (2000), do members of minority ethnic groups. While members of minority ethnic groups are often held responsible for the introduction of drugs into a country or community, the evidence would suggest that when they fall prey to addiction or to other drug-related difficulties, they are under-serviced by the state. A study conducted on British drug policy highlighted that the specific drug-related needs of minorities rarely get the attention they deserve. Yet, the evidence suggests that consumption patterns are different within specific minority ethnic groups when compared with other sectors of the population. A study on the drug consumption patterns of members of the Travelling community in this country highlights differences in the age at which consumption starts, gender differences and types of drugs consumed from the settled population.

Racial stereotypes also come quickly to mind when the subject of drug use is raised (Bourgois, 1995). While Khan and others challenge the notion that members of minority ethnic groups are more likely to use illicit drugs, they do acknowledge different patterns in their drug use and the need for a different response. That response is not happening at present. One group that is more likely to use drugs is gay men and Tierney's (2002) account suggests high levels of polydrug use. Another group where high levels of drug use is to be found is amongst prisoners, despite the difficulties attached to getting drugs in and out of prison.

The evidence also indicates that women and men experience drugs differently and so drug policies need to reflect that. While it still remains true to say that illicit drug use is predominantly the preserve of men, more and more women in Ireland are beginning to experiment. The number of female drug users is increasing at a faster rate than it is for males (Geoghegan et al., 1999), a trend that is also to be found from international studies. Not everybody is in agreement with what this means. One commentator (Henderson, 1999) sees this as part of a wider process of women coming more to the fore in society, taking more control of their lives as a statement of their independence and empowerment and freeing themselves from patriarchal power structures. Others are not convinced.

What Henderson and others have contributed to the debate is an awareness of the different ways in which drug use affects women and men and the need for policy-makers to reflect that.

They highlight the need for drug policies to be gender-proofed and gender-mainstreamed. In "Mainstreaming Equality between Women and Men in Ireland", the Department of Justice, Equality and Law Reform outlines how equality between women and men can be developed:

> When mainstreaming a policy, policy makers can ask, at all stages of policy development — when we make a policy, are we accidentally contributing to some inequalities? If we change our decisions in some manner, can we help to address inequalities? Instead of solving problems later, it is possible to be pro-active the whole way through the policy making process. This helps to avoid accidentally creating or compounding inequalities. (Department of Justice, Equality and Law Reform, 2000, p. 7)

Not only must policy-makers in all areas develop gender-fair policies, but they must also identify indicators or measures to identify the strengths and weaknesses of those policies. Gender impact assessment involves the review of policies to ascertain their differential impact on women and men. This applies to drug policies as it does to every other policy area.

Speaking in 1999 at the gender mainstreaming conference in Cavan, the Taoiseach Bertie Ahern stated that gender mainstreaming "requires us to rethink established norms and behaviours and to adjust our perceptions, attitudes and behaviour" (Ahern, 1999). Recognising that such change is difficult, the Taoiseach went on to say that gender mainstreaming was an important outcome from the fourth UN World Conference on Women in Beijing in 1995 and has been enshrined in Article 3 of the Treaty of Amsterdam.

If there is a legislative requirement for drugs to be gender-proofed, the evidence above would suggest that this proofing needs to be extended to include age, social class, sexual orientation, ethnicity and race so that we can rethink our established norms and behaviours and adjust our perceptions, attitudes and behaviour.

One of the major dilemmas confronting policy-makers is centred on how to respond to the current position. Significant work encompassing a range of interventions has been done in this and other countries with a view to preventing the onset of or reducing the harm caused by drug use. Many of these approaches have strong ideological perspectives and reflect how particular societies view the whole debate on drugs and drug users in particular.

Each of these interventions can be located somewhere along a continuum that has prevention/abstinence at one end and harm reduction at the other. The evidence as summarised by Morgan (2000) is that there is no one solution, no secret formula and no magical answers. Rather, there are various underlying factors, various influences, and various substances that require multifaceted responses. These responses can only enable us manage increasing drug use.

What is clear is that the centuries-old desire for psychoactive substances, whether as an act of desperation or celebration, will always remain part of the human condition. There is no one answer that will control or stop the tide of consumption. There is no King Canute.

REFERENCES

Aart Scholte, J. (2000), *Globalization: A Critical Introduction*, Macmillan Press, London.

Abozaglo, P. (2001), *Colombia*, Trócaire, Maynooth, Co. Kildare.

Ahern, B. (1999), "Mainstreaming Gender Equality", speech by An Taoiseach at the Mainstreaming Gender Equality Conference, Slieve Russell Hotel, Cavan, 29 April. www.gov.ie/taoiseach/press/current/29-04-99

Ahern, B. (2001) "Speech by the Taoiseach, Mr Bertie Ahern TD" at the launch of National Drugs Strategy in the Press Centre, Government Buildings, Dublin, 10 May. www.gov.ie/taoiseach/press/current/10-05-01.htm

Amnesty International (2001), *Racism in Ireland: The Views of Black and Ethnic Minorities*, Amnesty International, Dublin.

Anderson, J.L. (1997), *Che Guevara: A Revolutionary Life*, Bantam Books, New York.

Bacik, I, Kelly, A., O'Connell, M., and Sinclair, H. (1998), "Crime and Poverty in Dublin: An Analysis of the Association between Community Deprivation, District Court Appearance and Sentence Severity" in Bacik, I., and O' Connell, M. (eds.), *Crime and Poverty*, Round Hall Sweet & Maxwell, Dublin.

Barker, J. (1998), "Thunder and Silence in Drug Treatment: Four Nations in Moral Concert" in Klingemann, H., and Hunt, G., *Drug Treatment Systems in an International Perspective: Drugs Demons and Delinquents*, Sage Publications, London.

BBC News (2003), "Profile of Nicholas Soames", http://news.bbc.co.uk

Belkin, L. (2001), "Freed from federal restrictions, pharmaceutical companies are flooding television with ads for prescription drugs. What does it mean for our health care when serious medicine is marketed like soap?", *Mother Jones*, April.

Blair, T., "The Prime Minister's Broadcast of Friday 18 February 2000". www.number-10.gov.uk/default.asp?pageID=1082

Blair, T., "The Prime Minister's Broadcast of Friday 10 March 2000". www.number-10.gov.uk/default.asp?pageID=1246

Blair, T., "The Prime Minister's Broadcast of Friday 09 April 2001". www.number-10.gov.uk/news.asp?NewsId=1997

Bloor, M and Wood, F. (1998), *Addictions and Problem Drug Use: Issues in Behaviour, Policy and Practice*, Jessica Kingsley Publishers, London.

Blunkett, D., "Blunkett to Focus on the Menance of Hard Drugs", Home Office Press Release. www.homeoffice.gov.uk/drugs/press-release-23.10.01.htm

Blunkett, D., Speech to the House of Commons, 10 July 2002, Westminster, London. www.publications.parliament.uk/pa/cm200102/cmhansrd/cm020710/.../20710-06.ht

Borger, J. and Hodgson, M. (2001), "A plane is shot down and the US proxy war on drug barons unravels", *The Guardian*, Saturday, 2 June.

Bourgois, P. (1995), *In Search of Respect: Selling Crack in El Barrio*, Cambridge University Press, Cambridge.

Bowden, M. (2001), *Killing Pablo*, Atlantic Books, London.

Brennock, M. (2003), "PDs' radical agenda resets parameters of political debate", *Irish Times*, 5 April.

Brook, J.S. and Brook, D.W. (1996), "Risk and Protective Factors for Drug Use" in McCoy, C.B., Metsch, L.R., and Inciardi, J.A.. (eds.), *Intervening with Drug Involved Youth*, Sage Publications, London.

Browne, R., Keating, S., and O'Connor, J. (1998), "Sexual Abuse in Childhood and Subsequent Illicit Drug Abuse in Adolescence and Early Childhood", *Irish Journal of Psychological Medicine*, Vol. 15, No. 4.

Bryan, A., Moram, R., Farrell, E., and O'Brien, M. (2000), *Drug Related Knowledge, Attitudes and Beliefs in Ireland: Report of a Nationwide Survey*, Drug Misuse Research Division, Health Research Board, Dublin.

Bullington, B. (1998), "America's Drug War: Fact or Fiction?" in Coomber, R. (ed.), *The Control of Drugs and Drug Users: Reason or Reaction*, Harwood Academic Publishers, United Kingdom.

Butler, S. (2002), *Alcohol, Drugs and Health Promotion in Modern Ireland*, Institute of Public Administration, Dublin.

Byrne, P. (2001), "Address by Garda Commissioner Patrick Byrne at the Patrick McGill Summer School at Glenties, Co. Donegal", 14 August.

Carlen, P. and Morgan, R. (1999), *Crime Unlimited? Questions for the 21st Century*, Macmillian Press Ltd., London.

Carrol, D., Foley, B., Hickson, F., O'Connor, J., Quinlan, M., Sheehan, B., Watters, R., and Weatherburn, P. (2000), *Vital Statistics Findings from the All-Ireland Gay Men's Sex Survey 2000*, Gay Health Network, Dublin.

Centre for International Policy (2003), "The Contents of the Colombia Aid Package", http:www.ciponline.org

Central Statistics Office (1999), "Census of Industrial Production Provisional Results, 1999", Central Statistics Office, Dublin.

Chetley, A. (1995), *Problem Drugs*, Zed Books, London.

Chomsky, N. (1989), *The Culture of Terrorism*, Pluto Press, London.

Chomsky, N. (2000), "The Colombian Plan: April 2000". Zmag http://www.zmag.org/ZMAG/articles/chomskyjune2000.htm

CIIR (Catholic Institute for International Relations) (1991), "Narcotics and Development Discussion Paper No. 1", Cannonbury Yard, London.

CityWide (1998), "Community Policing Conference", 20 June (unpublished).

Cleary, C. (2001), "Teens claim Martin's 'preachy' website is out of touch", *Sunday Tribune*, 15 July.

Clinton, B. (1997), "Remarks by the President in Apology for the Study done in Tuskegee", Office of the Press Secretary, Washington.

COCAD (1999), "Report of the Estate Management Seminar & Workshop" Dublin. Coalition of Communities Against Drugs.

Combat Poverty Agency (2001), *Tackling Drugs at Local Level: A Policy Perspective*, Combat Poverty Agency, Dublin.

Combat Poverty Agency (1999), *Annual Report 1998*, Combat Poverty Agency, Dublin.

Coomber, R. (1998), *The Control of Drugs and Drug Users: Reason or Reaction*, Harwood Academic Publishers, United Kingdom.

CORI (2001), "News Release" 6 June. www.cori.ie

Cortez Hurtado, R. (1993), "Coca, Cocaine and International Politics: A View from Bolivia", in *The International Drug Trade: Finding the West Country Connection*, A CIIR/Bristol University Seminar, Bristol University, 25 September.

Council of Ministers. (1997), *The Treaty of Amsterdam, the Treaty on European Union, the Treaties Establishing the European Communities and certain Related Acts signed at Amsterdam, 2 October 1997*, Office for Official Publications, Luxembourg.

Cox, G. and Lawless, M. (2000), *Making Contact: Evaluation of a Syringe Exchange Programme*, Merchant's Quay Project, Dublin.

Cusack, J. (2000), "Dáil hearing told new prison health regime is needed to deal with drugs", *Irish Times*, 9 November.

Davenport-Hines, R. (2001), *The Pursuit of Oblivion: A Social History of Drugs*, Phoenix Press, London.

Dembo, R., and Rivers, J.E., (1996), "Juvenile Health Service Centres: An Exciting Time to Intervene with Drug Involved and Other High Risk Youth", in McCoy, C.B., Metsch, L.R., and Inciardi J.A. (eds.), *Intervening with Drug Involved Youth*, Sage Publications, London.

Department of Education and Science (1992), *Education for a Changing World*, Department of Education and Science, Dublin.

Department of Education and Science (1995), *Charting our Education Future*, Department of Education and Science, Dublin

Department of Education and Science (2000a), *Exploring Masculinities*, Department of Education and Science, Dublin.

Department of Education and Science (2000b), *Junior Cycle Social, Personal & Health Education*, Government Publications, Dublin.

Department of Health (1994), *Shaping a Healthier Future*, Stationery Office, Dublin.

Department of Justice, Equality and Law Reform (2000), "Mainstreaming Equality between Women and Men in Ireland", Department of Justice, Equality and Law Reform, Dublin.

Department of An Taoiseach (1996), *First Report of the Ministerial Task Force on Measures to Reduce the Demand for Drugs*, Government Publications, Dublin.

Department of Tourism, Sport & Recreation (2001), *National Drugs Strategy 2001–2008*, Government Publications, Dublin.

Derks, J.T.M., Hoekstra, M.J., and Kaplan, C.D. (1998), "Integrating Care, Cure, and Control: The Dutch Treatment Systems in the Netherlands", in Klingemann, H. and Hunt, G. (eds.), *Drug Treatment Systems in an International Perspective: Drugs Demons and Delinquents*, Sage Publications, London.

Desmond, B. (2000), *Finally and In Conclusion*, New Island, Dublin.

Dillon, L. (2001), *Drug Use Among Prisoners: An Exploratory Study*, The Health Research Board, Dublin.

Dixon, P. (1998), *The Truth about Drugs: Facing the Big Issue of the Millennium*, Hodder & Stoughton, London.

dooyoo, "*Trainspotting* (1996) reviews, ratings guide", www.dooyoo.co.uk

Dorgan, M. and McDonnell, O. (1997), "Conversing on Class Activism: Claiming Our Space in Feminist Politics", in *Irish Journal of Feminist Studies*, Volume 2, Issue 1, Summer.

Dorn, N. and Lee, M. (1999), "Drugs and Policing in Europe: from Low Streets to High Places", in South, N. (ed.), *Drugs, Culture Controls and Everyday Life*, Sage Publications, London.

Drug Education Matters (2001), "Blowing the Whistle on Police — Do They Make Good Educators?" *Drug Education Matters*, Issue 10, Spring.

Economist.com, "Drugs, war and democracy", 25 June 2001 www.economist.com/displayStory.cfm?Story_ID=576197

Esperanza Productions, *Race to the Bottom*, Documentary Broadcast on TG4, 19 December 2002.

European Monitoring Centre for Drugs and Drug Addiction (2000), *Annual Report on the State of the Drug Problem in the European Union*, Office for the Official Publications of the European Communities, Luxembourg.

European Monitoring Centre for Drugs and Drug Addiction (2001), "Drugnet Europe No. 28", European Monitoring Centre for Drugs and Drug Addiction, Lisbon, March-April 2001 and July-August 2001. www.emcdda.org

European Parliament, Session Document 1999–2004. B5 – 0541/2002 23/12/02.

European Union Commission (1999), "Communication from the Commission to the Council and the European Parliament on a European Union Action Plan to Combat Drugs (2000–2004), Brussels, 26 May.

European Union (1999), "Decision of the European Parliament and the Council of Ministers on a Multiannual Community Action Plan on Promoting Safer Use of the Internet", 276/199/EC L.33, 6 February, Office for Official Publications, Luxembourg.

Fitzgerald, G. (1991), *All in a Life*, Dublin, Gill and Macmillan.

Flynn, P. (2001), *Social Consequences of and Responses to Drug Misuse in Member States: A Report for the Social, Health and Family Affairs Committee of the Council of Europe*, Council of Europe, Strasbourg.

Fullan, M.G., and Stiegelbaur, S. (1992), *The New Meaning of Educational Change*, Cassell, London.

Garda Síochána (1997), Annual Report 1996, An Garda Síochána, Dublin.

Geoghehan, T., O'Shea, M., and Cox, C. (1999), "Gender Differences in Characteristics of Drug Users Presenting to a Dublin Syringe Exchange", *Irish Journal of Psychological Medicine*, Vol. 16, No. 4.

George, S. (1992), *The Debt Boomerang*, Pluto Press, London.

Gibbons, F. (2001), "*Porno*: Five Years on from *Trainspotting*", in *The Guardian*, 22 August.

Giddens, A. (1993), *Sociology*, Polity Press, Cambridge.

Gleeson, J. (1989), "Junior Certificate: Trojan Horse or Mickey Mouse?", *Compass*, Vol. 18, No. 2.

Government of Ireland (1997), "Housing (Miscellaneous Provisions) Act, 1997", Government Information Services, Dublin.

Government of Ireland (2000), *Ireland: National Development Plan 2000–2006*, Government Publications, Dublin.

Government of the UK, *Tackling Drugs to Build a Better Britain*. www.officialdocuments.co.uk/document/cm39/3945/statement.htm

Harrison, L.D., and Pottieger, A.E. (1996), "The Epidemiology of Drug Use Among American Youth", in McCoy, C.B., Metsch, L.R., and Inciardi, J.A., *Intervening with Drug Involved Youth*, Sage Publications, London.

Haskins, M. (2003), *Drugs: A User's Guide*, Ebury Press, London.

Health Promotion Unit (1997), *Understanding Drugs*, Department of Health, Dublin.

Henderson, S. (1999), "Drugs and Culture: the Question of Gender", in South, N. (ed.), *Drugs, Culture Controls and Everyday Life*, Sage Publications, London.

Hitchens, C. (2001), *The Trail of Henry Kissinger*, Verso, London.

Hunt, G. and Dong Sun, A.X. (1998), "The Drug Treatment System in the United States: A Panacea for the Drug War? in Klingemann, H. and Hunt, G. (eds.), *Drug Treatment Systems in an International Perspective: Drugs Demons and Delinquents*, Sage Publications, London.

Hurley, L. (1999), "Drugs and the Travelling Community", Pavee Point Travellers' Resource Centre, Dublin.

Hussey, G. (1990), *At the Cutting Edge: Cabinet Diaries 1982–1987*, Gill and Macmillan, Dublin.

Inciardi, J.A. (2000), "The Harm Reduction Roles of the American Criminal Justice System" in Incaiardi, J.A., and Harrison, L.D. *Harm Reduction — National and International Perspectives*, Sage Publications, London.

Inciardi, J.A. and Harrison, L.D. (2000), *Harm Reduction — National and International Perspectives*, Sage Publications, London.

Inglis, T. (1998), *Lessons in Irish Sexuality*, University College Dublin, Dublin.

International Information and Communication Division of the Ministry of Foreign Affairs, The Netherlands (2002), *Drugs: A Guide to Dutch Policy*, The Netherlands.

Irish Times, "Commercial Supplement", 29 September 2001.

Jelsma, M. (2001), *Vicious Circle: The Chemical and Biological "War on Drugs"*, Transnational Institute, Amsterdam.

Kelling, G.L., and Coles, C.M. (1996), *Fixing Broken Windows: Restoring Order and Reducing Crime in our Communities*, The Free Press, London.

Keogh, D. (1994), *Twentieth-Century Ireland — Nation and State*, Gill and Macmillan, Dublin.

Khan, K. (2000), "Mapping Available Information on Social Exclusion and Drugs, Focussing on 'Minorities' Across 15 EU member States", EMDDA.

Kiely, E. and Egan, E. (2000), *Drug Education: A Social and Evaluative Study*, The Cork Local Drugs Task Force, Cork.

Klingemann, H. and Hunt, G. (1998), *Drug Treatment Systems in an International Perspective: Drugs Demons and Delinquents*, Sage Publications, London.

Korf, D. J. and Buning, E.C. (2000), "Coffee Shops, Low Threshold Methadone and Needle Exchange: Controlling Illicit Drug use in the Netherlands" in Inciardi, J.A. and Harrison, L.D., *Harm Reduction — National and International Perspectives*, Sage Publications, London.

Lee, J.J. (1989), *Ireland 1912–1985: Politics and Society*, Cambridge University Press, Cambridge.

Letwin, O., Speech to the House of Commons, 10 July 2002, Westminster, London. www.publications.parliament.uk/pa/cm200102/cmhansrd/cm020710/.../20710-06.ht

London Drug Policy Forum (1996), *Dance Till Dawn — A Code of Practice on Health and Safety at Dance Venues*, London Drug Policy Forum, London.

Mac an Ghaill, M., Hanafin, J. and Conway, P. (2002), *Teachers, Materials and the Media: a Study of Exploring Masculinities in an International Context*, Department of Education and Science, Dublin.

McCabe, F. (1999), "Foreword" in Coveney, E., Murphy-Lawless, J., Redmond, D., and Sheridan, S., *Prevalence, Profiles and Policy: A Case Study of Drug Use in North Inner City Dublin*, North Inner City Drugs Task Force, Dublin.

McCoy, A. (1991), *Politics of Heroin: CIA Complicity in the Global Drug Trade*, Harper & Row Publishers, New York.

McCoy, C.B., Metsch, L.R., and Inciardi, J.A. (1996), *Intervening with Drug Involved Youth*, Sage Publications, London.

McDermott, P. (2000), "Reflections on British Drug Policy". Text of a speech delivered at the Methadone Alliance Conference, *Methadone and Beyond: Expanding and Exploring Drug Treatment Options*, 22 March, London. www.ukhra.org

MacGregor, S. (1999), "Medicine, Custom or Moral Fibre: Policy Responses to Drug Misuse" in South, N. (ed.), *Drugs, Culture Controls and Everyday Life*, Sage Publications, London.

MacGregor, S. and Smith, L. (1998), "The English Drug Treatment System: Experimentation or Pragmatism?" in Klingemann, H., and Hunt, G., *Drug Treatment Systems in an International Perspective: Drugs Demons and Delinquents*, Sage Publications, London.

MacPherson, W. (1999), *The Stephen Lawrence Inquiry: Report of an Inquiry by Sir William MacPherson of Cluny*, The Stationery Office, London.

McVeigh, R. (2002), "Between Reconciliation and Pacification: The British State and Community Relations in the North of Ireland", in *Community Development Journal Ireland, Corporatism and Community Development: Special Issue*, Volume 37, Number 1, January, Oxford University Press.

Memorandum for the President, From Roderick Hills: Scheduling of meeting re Invitation to Mrs Frank Olson and her three children to meet with the President, July 16, 1975, Gerald R. Ford Library.

Merchant's Quay Project (1999), *Annual Report*, Merchant's Quay, Dublin.

Mid-Western Health Board (1998), "Prostitution in the Mid West Region", Mid-Western Health Board, Limerick.

Millar, F. (2003) "Chilled by the Winds of War", *Irish Times*, 11 January.

Morgan, M. (2001), *Drug Use Prevention: Overview of Research*, National Advisory Committee on Drugs, Stationery Office, Dublin.

Morgan, M., Morrow, R., Sheehan, A.M. and Lillis, M. (1996), "Prevention of substance misuse: Rationale and effectiveness of the programme '*On My Own Two Feet*'", *Oideas: Journal of the Department of Education and Science*, Dublin.

Mott, J. and Bean, P. (1998), "The Development of Drug Control in Britain" in Coomber, R., *The Control of Drugs and Drug Users: Reason or Reaction*, Harwood Academic Publishers, United Kingdom.

Murji, K. (1998), "The Agony and the Ecstasy: Drugs, Media and Morality" in Coomber, R. *The Control of Drugs and Drug Users: Reason or Reaction*, Harwood Academic Publishers, United Kingdom.

Murphy, T. (1996), *Rethinking the War on Drugs in Ireland*, Cork University Press, Cork.

Murphy-Lawless, J. (2002), *Fighting Back: Women and the Impact of Drug Abuse on Families and Communities*, The Liffey Press, Dublin.

National Drugs Task Force (1996), *First Report of the Ministerial Task Force on Measures to Reduce the Demand for Drugs*, Department of Tourism, Sport and Recreation, Dublin.

National Drugs Task Force (1997), *Second Report of the Ministerial Task Force on Measures to Reduce the Demand for Drugs*, Department of Tourism Sport and Recreation, Dublin.

National Social Services Board (2000), *Directory of National Voluntary Organisations*, National Social Services Board, Dublin.

Netherlands Institute of Mental Health and Addiction (2001), "Drug Policy Fact Sheet", 15 July.
www.minjust.nl:8080/a_beleid/fact/cfact7.hmt

North American Congress on Latin America (2000), "Report on the Americas", Vol. XXXIV, No. 2, Sept/Oct.

O'Brien, M. and Moran, R. (1997), *Overview of Drug Issues in Ireland*, Health Research Board, Dublin.

O'Connell, S. (2001), "The Radical Alternative for Drug Addicts", *Irish Times: A Commercial Supplement*, 29 September.

O'Donoghue, J. (1997), "Speech in Seanad Éireann introducing The Criminal Justice No. 2 Bill", Seanad Debates, Official Report 9-12-97.

O'Donoghue, M. (1997), "Moving Forward Together: A Study of Community Needs in Our Lady of Lourdes Parish, Limerick City", Our Lady of Lourdes Community Services Group, Limerick.

O'Mahony, P. (1996), *Criminal Chaos: Seven Crises in Irish Criminal Justice*, Round Hall Sweet & Maxwell, Dublin.

O'Mahony, P. (2000), *Prison Policy in Ireland: Criminal Justice versus Social Justice*, Cork University Press, Cork.

O'Reilly, E. (undated), *Masterminds of the Right*, Attic Press, Dublin.

Orlandi, M.A. (1996), " Prevention Technologies for Drug Involved Youth" in McCoy, C.B. Metsch, L.R. and Inciardi, J.A. (eds.), *Intervening with Drug Involved Youth*, Sage Publications, London.

O'Shea, M. (1999), "The Computer Clubhouse" (unpublished).

O'Toole, F. (2003) "Law with a Dangerous Edge of Racism", *Irish Times*, 25 January.

Parker, H. (1999), "Illegal Leisure: Alcohol, Drugs and Regulation of Modern Youth" in Bloor, M., and Wood, F. (eds.), *Addictions and Problem Drug Use: Issues in Behaviour, Policy and Practice*, Jessica Kingsley Publishers, London.

Pilger, J. (1998), *Hidden Agendas*, Vintage, London.

Plant, M. and Plant, M. (1992), *Risk Takers, Alcohol, Drugs, Sex and Youth*, Routledge, London and New York.

Plant, M.A., Peck, D.F., and Samuel, E. (1985), *Alcohol, Drugs and School-Leavers*, Tavistock Publications Ltd, London.

Regan, C. (ed.) (2002), *80:20 — Development in an Unequal World*, 80:20 Educating and Acting for a Better World and Teachers in Development Education, Dublin.

Resnick, M. and Rusk, N. (1996), "The Computer Clubhouse: Preparing for Life in a Digital World".
http://llk.media.mit.edu/papers.1996/clubhouse/

Reverby, S. (2001), "More Fact than Fiction: Cultural Memory and the Tuskegee Syphilis Study", *The Hastings Centre Report*, Vol. 31, No. 5.

Rhodes, T. and Stimson, G.V. (1998), "Community Interventions Among Hidden Populations of Injecting Drug Users in the Time of AIDS in Bloor, M. and Wood, F. (eds.), *Addictions and Problem Drug Use: Issues in Behaviour, Policy and Practice*, Jessica Kingsley Publishers, London.

Riley, D. and O'Hare, P. (2000), "Harm Reduction: History, Definitions and Practice" in Inciardi, J.A. and Harrison, L.D., *Harm Reduction: National and International Perspectives*, Sage Publications, London.

Robson, P. (1994), *Forbidden Drugs: Understanding Drugs and Why People Take Them*, Oxford University Press, Oxford.

Rosenberger, L.R. (1996), *America's Drug War Debacle*, Ashgate Publishing Ltd., Aldershot.

Ruddle, H., Prizeman, G. and Jaffro, G. (2000), *Evaluation of Local Drugs Task Force Projects: Experiences and Perceptions of Planning and Implementation*, Brunswick Press, Dublin.

Shapiro, H. (1999), "Cultures, Forms and Representations: Dances with Drugs" in South, N. (ed.), *Drugs, Culture Controls and Everyday Life*, Sage Publications, London.

Shelder, J., and Block, J. (1990), "Adolescent Drug Use and Psychological Health" in *American Psychologist*, 45.

Sher, K.J. (1991), *Children of Alcoholics*, University of Chicago Press, Chicago.

Shiner, M. and Newburn, T. (1999), "Taking Tea with Noel: The Place and Meaning of Drug use in Everyday Life" in South, N. (ed.), *Drugs, Culture Controls and Everyday Life*, Sage Publications, London.

Shorrock, T. (2002), "The Big Guns", *New Internationalist*, 347.

South, N. (1999), *Drugs, Culture Controls and Everyday Life*, Sage Publications, London.

Southern Health Board (1999), *Developing Policy on Alcohol, Tobacco and Drug Use Guidelines for Schools*, Southern Health Board, Cork.

Spears, C. and Ó Loinsigh, G. (2000), "Plan Colombia — Diseased Proposal", *Focus*, Aug/Sept.

Spruit, I. (1998), "Deviant or Just Different?" in Bloor, M. and Wood, F. (eds.), *Addictions and Problem Drug Use: Issues in Behaviour, Policy and Practice*, Jessica Kingsley Publishers, London.

Standing Conference on Drug Abuse (UK) (1999), *Drug Education and Prevention Handbook*, Health Education Authority, London.

Stimson, G. (2000), "Blair Declares War: The Unhealthy State of UK Drug Policy", Text of a speech delivered at the Methadone Alliance Conference *Methadone and Beyond: Expanding and Exploring Drug Treatment Options*, London, 22 March. www.ukhra.org

Supply Control Committee of the Inter-Agency Drugs Project (North Inner City Dublin) (1998), "New Community Policing and Estate Management Model", *Poverty Today*, No. 39 (March–April).

Tate, W. (2001), "Repeating Past Mistakes: US Role in Counterinsurgency in Colombia", *Third World Resurgence*, January–February.

Tierney, P. (2002), "High as a Kite", *Attitude*, July.

Transnational Institute (2001), "Europe and Plan Colombia", Drugs & Conflict Debate Paper No. 1, April. www.tni.org/drugs/research/plcoleu.htm

Transnational Institute (2001), "Fumigation and Conflict in Colombia in the Heat of Debate", Drugs & Conflict Debate Paper No. 2, September. www.tni.org/reports/drugs/debate2.htm

Transnational Institute (2001), "Merging Wars: Afghanistan, Drugs and Terrorism", Drugs & Conflict Debate Paper No. 3, November. www.tni.org/reports/drugs/debate3.htm

Transnational Institute (2002), "A Failed Balance: Alternative Development and Eradication", Drugs & Conflict Debate Paper No. 4, March. www.tni.org/reports/drugs/debate4.htm

Tucker, V. (1996), 'Health, medicine and Development: A Field of Cultural Struggle'. The European Journal of Development Research Vol. 8 No. 2.

United Nations (2001), *World Drugs Report 2000*, United Nations Publications, New York.

United Nations Office for Drug Control and Crime Prevention (UNODCCP) (2002), *Global Illicit Drug Trends*, United Nations Publications. New York.

UNAIDS/WHO (2002), *AIDS Epidemic Update December 2002*, United Nations Publications, New York.

van de Kook, De Wereld (1993), "The Failure of Good Intentions", Discussion Paper No. 5, CIIR (Catholic Institute for International Relations), Cannonbury Yard, London.

van Muijlwijk, M. (1999), *Be Equal Be Different*, Age Action Ireland and Outhouse, Dublin.

Wacquant, L.J.D., (1993), "Urban Outcasts: Stigma and Division in Black American Ghetto and the French Urban Periphery", *International Journal of Urban and Regional Research*, Vol. 17, No. 3.

Walton, S. (2001), *Out Of It: A Cultural History of Intoxication*, Hamish Hamilton, London.

Welsh, I. (1999), *Trainspotting*, Vintage, London.

White House, The, Statement of the President Gerald R. Ford Library, 12 October 1976.

Wilson, J.Q. (1996), "Foreword" in Kelling, G.L. and Coles, C.M., *Fixing Broken Windows: Restoring Order and Reducing Crime in our Communities*, The Free Press, London.

Woodiwiss, M. (1998), "Reform, Racism and Rackets: Alcohol and Drug Prohibition in the United States" in Coomber, R., *The Control of Drugs and Drug Users: Reason or Reaction*, Harwood Academic Publishers, United Kingdom.

World Bank (2001), *World Development Report 2000/2001: Attacking Poverty*, Oxford University Press, Oxford.